THE ULTIMATE GUIDE
TO CALLING AND DECOYING
WATERFOWL

Books by Monte Burch

Field Dressing and Butchering Deer
Field Dressing and Butchering Upland Birds, Waterfowl, and Wild Turkeys
Field Dressing and Butchering Rabbits, Squirrels, and Other Small Game
Field Dressing and Butchering Big Game
The Field & Stream All-Terrain-Vehicle Handbook
Denny Brauer's Jig Fishing Secrets
Denny Brauer's Winning Tournament Tactics
Black Bass Basics
Guide to Calling & Rattling Whitetail Bucks
Guide to Successful Turkey Calling
Guide to Calling & Decoying Waterfowl
Guide to Successful Predator Calling
Pocket Guide to Seasonal Largemouth Bass Patterns
Pocket Guide to Seasonal Walleye Tactics
Pocket Guide to Old Time Catfish Techniques
Pocket Guide to Field Dressing, Butchering & Cooking Deer
Pocket Guide to Bowhunting Whitetail Deer
Pocket Guide to Spring & Fall Turkey Hunting
Guide to Fishing, Hunting & Camping Truman
The Pro's Guide to Fishing Missouri Lakes
Waterfowling, A Sportsman's Handbook
Modern Waterfowl Hunting
Shotgunner's Guide
Gun Care and Repair
Outdoorsman's Fix-It Book
Outdoorsman's Workshop
Building and Equipping the Garden and Small Farm Workshop
Basic House Wiring
Complete Guide to Building Log Homes
Children's Toys and Furniture
64 Yard and Garden Projects You Can Build
How to Build 50 Classic Furniture Reproductions
Tile Indoors and Out
The Home Cabinetmaker
How to Build Small Barns & Outbuildings
Masonry & Concrete
Pole Building Projects
Building Small Barns, Sheds & Shelters
Home Canning & Preserving (with Joan Burch)
Building Mediterranean Furniture (with Jay Hedden)
Fireplaces (with Robert Jones)
The Homeowner's Complete Manual of Repair and Improvement (with three others)
The Good Earth Almanac Series
Survival Handbook
Old-Time Recipes
Natural Gardening Handbook

THE ULTIMATE GUIDE TO CALLING AND DECOYING WATERFOWL

Tips and Tactics for Hunting Ducks and Geese

MONTE BURCH

The Lyons Press
Guilford, Connecticut
An imprint of The Globe Pequot Press

Copyright © 2002 by Monte Burch

First Lyons Press paperback edition, 2004

The Lyons Press is an imprint of The Globe Pequot Press.

10 9 8 7 6 5 4 3 2

Printed in the United States of America

ISBN 978-1-59228-523-5

Library of Congress Cataloging-in-Publication Data is available on file.

CONTENTS

INTRODUCTION

Waterfowling is one of the most exhilarating, exciting, frustrating, and challenging, yet enjoyable outdoor pastimes. To the true waterfowler it's more a way of life than a simple hobby. The birds themselves offer great mystery and beauty. The haunting sounds of migrating geese during a full-moon night, the elegance of big red-legged mallards dropping out of the sky after a long journey across North America are just some of the sights and sounds the waterfowler loves. The darting, fighter-jet maneuvering of teal or the streaking passes bluebills or buffleheads make by the blind offer challenging wingshooting, with the birds collected often a matter of luck as much as skill. Just as often the results are holes shot in the sky.

A good part of the appeal of waterfowling is just being there. Watching the beauty of a sunrise over the marsh, field, or open water is one of the great joys of waterfowling. Then there's the wildlife that inhabits the waterfowler's world, ranging from the tiny wren that feels a blind belongs to her, to the eagles, herons, muskrats, beavers, and many others.

Even the simplest of waterfowling is, however, rarely easy. Getting up from a warm bed, many hours before sunrise, to get to the hunting spot, then setting out decoys in frigid water, sitting in a blind or wrapped in camouflage on the cold ground, and waiting for the birds to come is certainly not for everyone. At the end of the hunt, it's time to retrieve the decoys and rebag them, often with frozen fingers and toes long gone numb. Then there's the very real danger of falling in the icy water. Waterfowlers die each year from mishaps, hypothermia, or drowning. But, as the saying goes, misery loves company, and waterfowlers love misery.

In addition to the hard work, many skills are needed for waterfowling. Knowing how to identify the different species is extremely important, as are good wingshooting skills. Knowing how to set out decoys and calling skills are also needed. If boating, safe boating skills are required, and then just good woodsman or waterman skills are necessary to read the conditions and match the hunting tactics to the conditions.

The money invested in gear and the time spent hunting are vast compared to the amount of meat harvested. Most waterfowlers, however, don't

Calling and decoying waterfowl is exciting, challenging, and extremely satisfying.

hunt purely for meat, but for the pleasure and challenge of the experiences. This is not to belittle the food garnered from duck or goose hunting. Dressed and prepared properly, waterfowl has been and can still be food fit for a king. Harvesting and preparing your own food is still a very necessary part of our hunting heritage as well.

I began as a youngster during the early 1950s and have been chasing ducks and geese for many years. I still get as excited as a newcomer to the game on opening day and when hard-worked birds finally commit to the decoys. I've been fortunate to hunt in many different locals and for many different types of waterfowl. I've also had the pleasure of hunting with many excellent pros, guides, and just serious waterfowlers. This book offers practical information on how to call and decoy the different types of waterfowl garnered from my own experiences as well as from many of my friends in the world of waterfowling.

1

HISTORY OF WATERFOWLING

The art of calling and decoying waterfowl has probably been around since humans became hunters. Egyptian hieroglyphics show waterfowl and fowling. Artifacts from American Indians include waterfowl decoys. An excellent example is a canvasback duck decoy made over a thousand years ago by a southwestern Indian and found in a cave. The body of the decoy is made of reeds bound tightly with flat rushes. The head and breast are colored with primitive pigments, and actual feathers are also fastened to the decoy to provide more realism.

The Tule Eaters, who were predecessors of the Northern Paiutes, were extremely innovative in decoying the great flights of waterfowl that migrated south in the fall and north in the winter. North American Indians of eastern America were also adept at fashioning decoys. In some instances the decoys were simply lumps of mud in shallow water, or rocks strategically placed, all to simulate birds. Dead birds were also propped up to look like live birds, a tactic many gunners still use today. It is thought, however, that the Tule Eaters also used mounted skins stuffed with dried grass placed on shore, or even on floating platforms. The reed bird decoys, however, provided more versatility and mobility. A number of these could be used to create the illusion of a whole flock of birds. The works of the long-ago decoy creator were discovered in protective baskets in the dry earth of a cavern floor in Lovelock Cave in Nevada in 1924. They are now located in the Museum of the American Indian in New York City.

American settlers quickly learned to copy the decoy tricks of the Indians. They discovered, however, that decoys made of skins and stuffed with grass or hay quickly deteriorated. As a result gunners began carving wooden decoys in the late 17th century. Carved of solid white cedar or pine, the decoys were quite primitive and called "blocks" due to their shape. They were also called "stools" after the European practice of fastening a live pigeon to a movable perch or pole as a lure or "stool" to attract other pigeons. Hence the name *stool pigeon*.

Along the Atlantic Coast gunners hunting scoter or eider sea ducks attached these blocks or stools in long lines to the back of their boats, and the tactic became known as "tolling" from the ancient term *tolling the death knell*. The gunners using the practice were commonly called tollers.

The word *decoy* actually is a contraction of a Dutch word *EndeKooy*, which was a cage or trap used to trap waterfowl before the use of firearms. By the early 1800s stool making was becoming an honorable profession along the upper Atlantic Coast. As many as 500 decoys were often employed on many of the better gunning flats in the area. By the mid-1800s decoy carvers began to make their blocks more lifelike with painted plumage and more detailed carvings. They also began to personalize their decoys more, adding certain style touches. Regional decoys evolved due to local conditions. For instance, gunners of the Barnegat Bay area of New Jersey, who were using large numbers of decoys in their sets, began to create hollow decoys that were lighter in weight and easier to carry. These decoys also had undersized bodies and oversized heads. Decoys from around the Stratford, Connecticut, area were designed for the vast marshes located at the mouth of the Housatonic River. They were created with overhanging breasts, which allowed the decoy to ride the slush ice that came down the river in both the spring and fall shooting periods. Very small decoys came about for gunners who wanted to hide the decoys in their pockets when violating the law against Sunday hunting.

By the latter part of the 19th century small factories were turning out thousands of decoys to meet the demands of the increasing number of amateur hunters, as well as the professional or market hunters. Some of the most famous included the Stevens Company of Weedsport, New York, the Dodge and Mason Companies from Detroit, Michigan, and the American Company from Illinois. Other innovations included a rubber decoy in 1867 and a patented honking decoy with a bellows operated by wave action. Tip-up decoys appearing like feeding ducks also came on the market. In addition, decoys began to be made of other materials including rubber, plastic, balsawood, cork, pressed paper, and composition board as well as tenite. The last part of the 19th century saw the great era of market gunning, as well as marked increases in private gunning. In 1846, one gunner from Chesapeake Bay bagged 1,000 canvasbacks. They were the most preferred for the market due to their taste, with redheads and bluebills the next choices.

Congress passed the Federal Migratory Bird Law in 1913 prohibiting spring shooting and also the shipment of waterfowl for sale. In 1919 the Federal Migratory Bird Treaty Act tried to prohibit the sale of wildfowl between the United States and Canada, but the prohibition was not really enforced until 1920.

That was the end of the market gunners. Many of these famous gunners had also become excellent decoy carvers. Charles E. ("Shang") Wheeler of Stratford, Connecticut, was one of the most well known. Harry Shourdes of Tuckerton, New Jersey, was also a very prolific decoy carver, supposedly carving more than 2,000 decoys a year.

Although decoy carving for working blocks was becoming obsolete, decoy carving as an art form was growing in popularity. In 1923 the first decoy carving championship was held in Bellport, Long Island. Wheeler won the grand championship with a now famous gray mallard decoy that is on display in the Shelburne Museum.

Today working decoys are mostly molded of plastic or sometimes carved of cork. I did have the fortune to hunt with a $24,000 spread of working blocks carved by a young man named Mike Kent several years ago. Mike succumbed at a young age to liver cancer, but his work is a legacy of today's decoy carvers. Decoy carving as an art is bigger and better than ever, as is collecting the old-time decoys.

The history of calls is just as interesting. The Native Americans were extremely adept at mimicking the sounds of animals and birds, including waterfowl. And it's unknown who made the first duck calls for their own use. According

Waterfowl decoys and calls are a major part in our hunting heritage. Early decoys have become major collector items, while carvers today still create decoys as "art."

to Howard Harlan and W. Crew Anderson, coauthors of *Duck Calls: An Enduring American Art*, the first commercial duck call, a tongue-pincher-style call, was introduced in 1854, then in 1870, Elam Fisher was awarded the first U.S. patent on a duck call, also a tongue-pincher style. It is believed that Fred Allen, of Monmouth, Illinois, probably made the first modern-style duck call with a barrel, stopper, and reed in 1863. From that time on until 1880, other Illinois call makers, including C. W. Grubbs and G. Patterson, were also influential in producing the Illinois River–style call. These calls consisted of a barrel, a round cork-wedge block, a straight tone board, and a curved metal reed.

Victor Glodo, another early call maker and market hunter on Reelfoot Lake in Tennessee, created the Reelfoot-style call in 1881, setting the style of today's modern duck calls. Around the turn of the century came Kuhlemeier's hard rubber call with rubber reed and rounded-off tone board. A number of other call makers continued to improve on these early calls. Then in 1957 George Yentzen and Jim Fernandez created the famous Yentzen double-reed call. These days numerous call manufacturers produce a wide variety of duck and goose calls.

2

TYPES OF CALLS

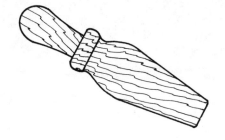

The flock of mallards was making another maddeningly slow circle behind the blind when my hunting partner, Eddie Stevenson of Remington, whispered, "pintails." Our guide continued his mallard talk and I grabbed the Flambeau pintail whistle on my lanyard and added in the thin, reedy-sounding whistles. The mallards made a final swing in front of the sunken blind and began to drop into the decoys. We let them come in, and they were almost immediately followed by the pintails. A flurry of shots and we began high-fiving. Three mallards and one bull pintail. Settled back in the blind admiring the brilliant colors on the beautiful bird, we heard the haunting *krrrr-onk* of a snow goose. Sure enough, a single, and very lost, snow goose was headed our way. We all three grabbed snow goose calls and went to work. Moments later Eddie raised his Remington 1100 and a brilliant white snow goose tumbled in front of the blind.

One of the reasons for our success was that we had been ready for almost any waterfowl species with several different types of calls. The wide array of waterfowl calls available today, however, makes choosing calls seem daunting.

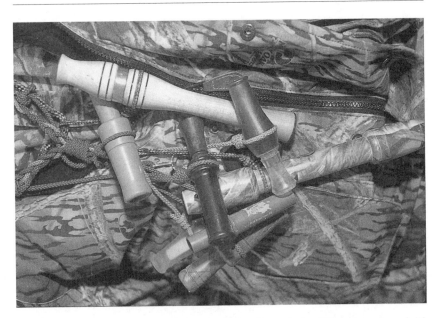

A wide array of waterfowl calls is available, with calls made for different species, of different materials and different configurations.

Waterfowl calls include calls for mallards and other puddle ducks, pintails, teal, wood ducks, and other "whistlers," calls for diver ducks, and goose calls for Canada geese, specklebellies, snows, and blues. Waterfowl calls are made of a wide variety of woods, molded plastics, and molded or turned acrylics. Each type of call has its own uses, and it's important to match the call to the hunting situation. Most waterfowlers carry several different calls with them while hunting. Some calls can become waterlogged or clogged up during damp or cold weather. This usually happens right when a flock of ducks is seriously working your blocks and you need to switch to a spare. Using several different calls with different tones and sounds can also create more variety in your calling and be more of an enticement to extremely wary waterfowl.

Waterfowl calls are extremely personal. Some are easy to blow, some are hard to blow, some create softer sounds, some are louder, some have high-pitched sounds, some have lower, more guttural sounds. There really is no way you can pick a packaged call off the shelf or rack and know it's the right call for you. You have to experiment with a variety of calls to find the one or ones that you can use the most effectively.

DUCK CALLS

Most duck calls are designed to imitate the quacking and feed chuckling sounds of mallards and other puddle ducks because all ducks will respond to these sounds. Although hundreds of duck calls are on the market, they basically all work in the same manner. A hollow mouthpiece has a reed fitted into it, and the reed is held in place with a "stopper" of some sort. This assembly is then inserted into a barrel. The barrel and mouthpiece have been traditionally turned on a wooden lathe using a variety of woods. Almost any type of wood can be and probably has been used by manufacturers or amateur call makers. Hardwoods are the most common choice as they turn sharper or crisper on the lathe, finish smoother, and provide more of a deep sound. Bill Harper, friend and former owner and president of Lohman Game Call Company, several years ago created a number of custom calls for me from a variety of woods including walnut, cherry, cocobolo, hedge or Osage orange, and maple. Each and every call had a somewhat different sound. The harder or more dense the wood, the louder and higher pitched the call. For this reason, extremely dense woods—including such exotic woods as rosewood and zebrawood—are often

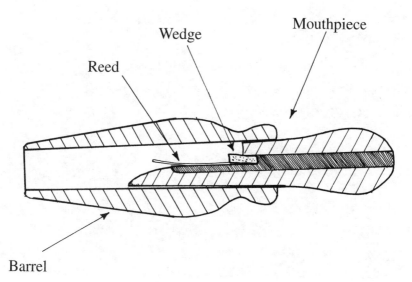

Reed

Wedge

Mouthpiece

Barrel

Most calls are made to imitate the sounds of mallard ducks and consist of a barrel, mouthpiece that fits into the barrel, reed, and stopper or wedge to hold the reed in place.

used. Unfortunately these woods are also prone to splitting. Call makers have solved that problem with brass retaining rings around the back of the barrel.

Today's manufactured wood calls are turned to extremely consistent tolerances of wood selected for its consistency, and they are hand tuned at the factory. Still, every call has a somewhat different sound. Again, you'll simply have to experiment to find the right call. Then there's the appearance of the call. Many waterfowl calls are true pieces of art using beautifully grained woods. Some custom calls even come with decorative carving added.

As a general rule, wood calls tend to absorb some of the sound and produce softer sounds than plastic and especially acrylic. For this reason wooden calls are more productive in flooded timber hunting, or areas where ducks may be closer at hand for calling. Plastic calls produce a bit sharper sound that carries more, but also can be softened if muffled down.

Olt has had a plastic call for many years, but it featured a cork stopper. Haydel's was the first to create an all-plastic call, all parts being something other than wood. "The advantage, and our main selling point when we first started our company, was the call could be submerged in water and still blow,"

Wood has been the traditional waterfowl call material. It is easy to work and produces great sounds.

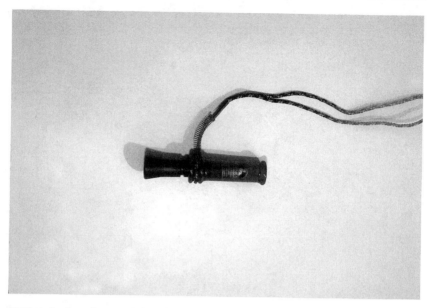

Molded-plastic calls are also available and produce somewhat sharper sounds. Shown here is the Primos Madam.

said Kelly Haydel. "That was our phrase, 'blows wet, not affected by moisture.' All the wood or cork parts will absorb moisture and that changes the pitch. On calls with the cork stopper, when the cork would get wet it would expand and cause more pressure on the reed and change the pitch of the call. So we eliminated the cork stopper by using a floating wedge made of plastic. The plastic wedge has an arch in it so that when you push it in, it adds the correct tension to the part and keeps everything nice and snug."

The acrylic calls are the most dense, and, for the most part, produce a higher-pitched, even sharper sound that is louder without as much pressure. They are the best choice if hunting open water or vast expanses of open marsh. They're also great for attracting ducks long distances over huge rice fields. Acrylic calls have become increasingly popular, and most call manufacturers offer full lines of acrylic calls. Both the plastic and acrylic calls are less affected by weather conditions and especially wet or moist weather. They tend to be more consistent in sounds in that respect.

A duck call is basically a reed musical instrument. The typical call consists of five parts, including: the barrel, which carries the sound; a "keg" that

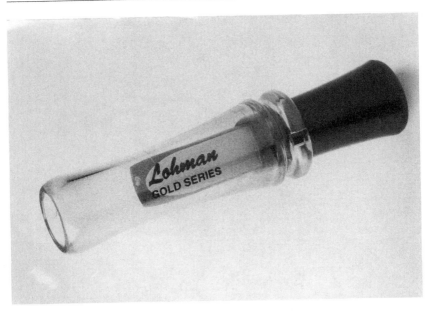

Acrylic calls produce even sharper or higher-pitched sounds. They are best for open waters and large marshes. (Photo courtesy Lohman)

holds the inner parts and carries the air across the reed to the barrel; a trough cut into the keg to produce a sound chamber; the reed, which can be made of different materials; and the wedge, which holds the reed in place. Modern duck calls are of three basic designs: the Arkansas, actually a Glodo type that originated in Illinois; the Cajun, sometimes called Louisiana or marsh call; and the Reelfoot. The Reelfoot design features a brass reed that is sometimes turned up on the end. These calls tend to be somewhat hard to blow.

The Cajun calls were once made of cane instead of wood because it was more readily available and in this instance the keg and trough are actually separate due to the choice of materials. The opening at the end of the keg is also larger on the Cajun calls, making them sound louder, more high pitched, and more raucous. Cajun-style calls were more commonly used on the open coastal marshes and are great for those windy days when a loud call is necessary. They are also a bit harder to blow.

The most common type of call design is the Arkansas, or Glodo style. In this design the trough and keg are one piece. With a smaller hole in the end of the keg, a somewhat softer sound is produced. These calls were more commonly used in the flooded timber along the Mississippi and White Rivers. Both the Reelfoot- and Louisiana-style calls tend to have longer barrels than the Arkansas style.

Reeds have been made of brass, hard rubber, Mylar, and these days of several high-tech "plastic" materials. Each also has its own type of sound. And, if that were not confusing enough, there's single- and double-reed calls. The old-time Yentzen call was unique in its time with a double reed, providing a totally different sound than other calls of the day.

Most manufacturers these days offer both single- and double-reed calls. Single-reed calls require the least amount of air pressure and effort to blow. They also have the widest tonal range, offering more versatility, and are often the choice of contest callers. Single-reed calls do have one drawback. If too much air or pressure is applied, they tend to stick, or if the reed is forced up off the sound board and the reed doesn't vibrate against the sound board, no sound is produced.

Although they require more air pressure to operate, and are not as versatile in the upper tonal range, double-reed calls tend to be easier for beginning callers because they are less prone to sticking. In other words, it's easier to

The Flex Tone calls are made of soft plastic with an acrylic reed assembly. The patented flexible barrel allows you to change the sound by simply squeezing the barrel.

make the different sounds without making mistakes. Single-reed calls require more precision in air control, and require more practice in learning how to "grunt" into the call to produce the sounds. With double-reed calls you can grunt as the experts do, or simply blow into them and get a passable sound.

Duck calls have different pitches as well. Some are high and raucous sounding, other lower and raspy. It's important to select the proper call for your particular hunting locale and situation. The higher-pitched calls are best for open water, especially those areas subjected to high winds. The lower-pitched calls are best for the more closed-in sloughs, rivers, and flooded timber situations. The tone of most duck calls is pretty well "set" with the position, thickness, and shape of the reed. Expert waterfowlers tune and reshape their calls to get a more "personalized" sound.

In addition to the standard mallard hen calls, drake calls, and gadwall calls, a wide variety of whistles are also available to entice pintails, teal, widgeon, and wood ducks. Drake/pintail and teal calls are available from several companies. The Hunter's Specialties Buck Gardner Duck Calling System is a little call that imitates the mallard drake, pintail, teal, wood duck, widgeon, plus a bobwhite quail and a redtail hawk. Other similar calls include the Sure-Shot Rascal 7–1 call, Primos Drake Whistle, Lohman Pintail Whistle and Wood Duck Call, Haydel's Magnum Pintail/Mallard Drake Call, and their Wood Duck Squealer and Blue-Wing Teal Calls.

GADWALL CALL

Due to the popularity of the "gray birds," Haydel's has produced an excellent-sounding gadwall call that creates the nasally sounding raspy quacks and feed chatter.

DIVER CALLS

Diver calls, such as the Lohman Diving Duck Call, are made like mallard calls but tuned differently to produce the purrs, brrrs, and barklike quacks of bluebills, canvasbacks, redheads, and other diving ducks.

SHAKER CALLS

If you have trouble creating feed chatter with a duck call, the bellows-style shaker call from Quaker Boy can make this chore easy. Simply shake the tube to create the sound.

Duck calls are available as single or double reed. Double-reed calls, shown here, are softer sounding, easier for beginners to learn to use. Single-reed calls are louder and require more control.

GOOSE CALLS

Four basic types of goose calls are available. First, there's the traditional "long-reed" goose call. There have been a tremendous number of long-reed calls made and they're still popular with many "traditionalists." This old-style call can still produce great sounds, but is not as versatile as many of the newer designs.

The next type is the tube goose call, originated by Harold Knight, the winner of three world championships. "It is a great call to use when the acoustics are still and quiet," said Knight. "It is a great call to use where you set up close to timber or where it is still with no wind blowing. The sound is so realistic the geese will come to it like on a string. It does, however, have two drawbacks—it's hard to master and you don't have a super volume with it. Other than that it is a deadly call on geese and I still use it every year."

The third type is the flute goose call. The flute call is a great call, especially for beginners, because you can blow it simply by puffing your cheeks. It's a good call just about anywhere, over water or fields. The P. S. Olt Company came up with their A-50, a "new-style" goose call they called the "flute call" way back in the 50's. "Now every call maker of any size and reputation makes a flute goose call," said James R. Olt of the P. S. Olt Company. The flute call utilizes a different design of the reed and reed bass (the contoured part, with a groove that the reed sits on). And very important, the main air passage chamber is behind the reed assembly instead of in front of it, as in most conventional goose calls. The result is a call that sounds much more like a Canada goose. The high notes are not as shrill and the low notes not as guttural. And you can make all sorts of clucks and double clucks and come-back calls with the flute call in addition to the longer greeting calls. Sounds that are not possible with a conventional goose call—at least in most caller's hands.

"The Lohman Flute Goose Call was designed by Mike Weller to produce the full range in sounds," said Brad Harris, public relations director of Outland Sports. "It can produce any known sound a goose can make.

"A problem that has existed with flute-type calls is callers learning how to blow them to make the call break over properly. The Lohman Choke System consists of four interchangeable rubber 'chokes' with openings of different sizes that restrict the air flow, and changing the choke rings allows the caller to match his air flow to the restriction of the choke needed to cause the call to break over the easiest into the two-note honk."

Whistle calls are available for species such as teal, pintails, widgeon, and wood ducks. They can be used to produce the titters and whistling sounds of these species.

A number of other manufacturers now offer flute-type goose calls, including Sean Mann calls from Eastern Shoreman, Haydel's Big River, Tim Grounds, Faulk's, and Mallardtone.

A somewhat similar call is the short-reed goose call. "It's the most popular call out right now," said Harold Knight. "Our Double Cluck Plus uses the same 'short-reed' concept as a flute call. Except some of the flute calls, like the Olt, are extended out to give a 'flutier' sound. I came out with the first beveled megaphone look on manufactured calls, where it's got a bell out on the end. There are similarities, but a lot of differences as well. The Magnum Clucker Goose Call is also a short-reed concept and similar to the Double Cluck, except it's a lot smaller call, extremely loud and extremely easy to blow, and that's what most folks want now, something easy to blow. I use these short-reed calls 90 percent of the time myself. They are very versatile and can give clucks, double clucks; you can get loud, soft, you can blow extremely fast with it. It's just a great call. There is a difference, however, in how you blow the calls. A flute call you blow mostly with your jaws, and this short-reed call you blow gutturally like a duck call. The short-reed call has a tone to it that is different, sharper. The flute call is softer, more muffled."

ELECTRONIC CALLS

The use of electronic calls has become legal with the advent of the conservation order to reduce overgrown snow goose populations. These calls can make easy work of creating the maddening din of thousands of geese, especially when mixed with manual calling. The Lohman Remote CD Wildlife Calling System is an excellent choice, along with their disk of snow geese feeding and flying.

LANYARDS

Good lanyards are necessary for keeping calls organized and up out of the mud and water. Any number of lanyards are available. The better lanyards have loops for more than one call. The Float-A-Call from Cabela's will prevent losing your calls if they drop in the water.

CALL MAKERS

Call manufacturers are also working to create more versatile calls that can produce a wider range of tones. Following are examples of some traditional and high-tech calls. All the manufacturers mentioned also produce a number of other calls as well.

The Flambeau Infinite Sound System calls are a series of patented, fully adjustable game calls that allow you to adjust the pitch and tone as desired. The system features a fully adjustable reed assembly that lets you adjust the tone and pitch of the call to match any duck hunting situation, from water to ice to open grain fields. A simple interlocking series of narrow grooves on the wedge and sound board allow you to move the adjustment wedge back and forth to create the different tones. The call is constructed of ABS plastic for extreme weather resistance and a rich, quality sound. Double O-rings prevent moisture from entering the call while firmly holding the parts together.

Flambeau features their ITS System in their Sweet Susie Double Reed Mallard Call. The versatile system allows you to instantly "tune" the call to

Drake calls produce the soft "buzzy" sounds of mallard drakes.

produce sounds for flooded timber and backwater sloughs, or the loud ringing sounds needed for open water. It comes with a double lanyard and a pair of O-ring seals and features a variable-tone hole to create the illusion of more than one hen calling by simply covering and uncovering the hole. The Single Reed Mallard Call creates the high-pitched come-back calls and also comes with the variable-tone hole. Also available from Flambeau is their Whistle Call that imitates the natural sounds of pintails, widgeon, teal, wood ducks, and even a mallard drake.

The Madam from Primos is a single-reed, Arkansas-style call with patented ditches incorporated on the trough that make it extremely easy to blow. The call also comes with two different-style reeds that can be interchanged for different sounds. One reed is designed as a working reed for hunting. The second reed has an entirely different shape for competition calling. Also available is their Power Drake and Duck Whistle. The design has increased volume to reproduce the sounds of pintails, widgeon, gadwall, greenwing teal, and mallard drake grunts. The larger design allows hunters with mustaches to use the call with ease.

Lohman, from Outland Sports, has combined over 60 years of experience with modern technology to produce a number of great calls constructed of unbreakable resin with a neoprene wedge to hold the uniquely designed reed for years of trouble-free use. The Marsh Master Premium Single Reed Duck Call produces championship-quality sounds with loud hail calls, demanding come-back calls, and sweet low-end coaxer calls. The Marsh Master Double Reed Duck Calls produce a full range of high- to low-end calls with a sweet double-reed sound. Lanyards are included. The Lohman Marsh Master Single Reed Duck Call is made of unbreakable resin and produces loud hail calls and demanding come-back calls. Also available from Outland Sports is the Big River Teal Call, which produces a raspy, soft sound of the blue-wing teal. Also from Outland Sports is the Lohman Gold Series Duck Call, an easy-to-blow call that has great sound and blows wet in all weather conditions. Like all Lohman Gold Series calls, it has an extra-loud sound.

The Big River Acrylic Duck Buster Elite, from Outland Sports, is made of solid acrylic. It produces great volume with minimal air, making it ideal for beginners and seasoned callers alike. Wooden Duck Buster models are also available. Big River Game Calls carries a full line of waterfowl calls in both wood and acrylic, and the calls are available with instruction cassettes. Three of the most popular duck calls include the wooden Duck Buster double reed; wooden Duck Master with either single, double, or double reed extra loud; and the formed Pro Magnum, double reed and double reed extra loud, also available in Advantage camo. Goose calls include the Terminator, designed with a higher-pitched sound, and a wide variety of Long Honker goose calls. The New Final Flight Goose Flute is one of the easiest-blowing flutes on the market.

The Buck Gardner Open Water Series, from Hunter's Specialties, is made of crystal-clear, polished acrylic, handmade and hand tuned. All feature a highly polished brass band, and four of the calls are open-water contest quality. All are extra loud. Also available is the Hunter Series of single-reed acrylic calls with brushed aluminum bands. The True Timber Custom Series are single-reed calls designed for less volume for close-in calling and are acrylic with brass bands. The Buck Gardner polycarbonate calls withstand bumps, scrapes, and moisture. Each features the Santoprene wedge. They include the Guide Series, Pro Series, Classic Series, and Signature Series in duck calls; Guide Series goose calls, and Pro and Pro Plus Goose Series.

Haydel's, world famous for their waterfowl calls, has a very large lineup of calls including their Variable Redleg Mallard call, a variable-tone version of

Haydel's gadwall call produces the nasally sounds of the "gray birds."

this successful 1999 call. The call has double O-rings and double reeds and comes with lanyard. A tuning hole allows the caller to sound like two different ducks. The Magnum Honker is a magnum version of the H-81 Canada call. The magnum barrels give smooth transitions while maintaining the volume needed in the field. The "Resonant Chamber" is designed to blow easy. "Just puff your cheeks while you blow"—it's that simple. The White Front Goose Call is constructed with double O-rings. The barrels have been designed to enhance and ease producing the clucks and yodels of "specks." Haydel's Calling Kit includes everything you need to get started calling ducks, including their Double Reed Mallard Call, a video that teaches not only mallard vocalization but all species of ducks and geese, and a visual aid that Eli Haydel used to teach all his sons. Haydel's also offers a Tune Up Kit with everything needed to tune their double-reed calls including four reeds, two O-rings, a wedge, and full instructions. The Waterfowl Workshop on cassette or CD is designed by Rod and Eli Haydel with instructions on how to blow Haydel waterfowl calls for all species of ducks.

P. S. Olt carries one of the largest lines of waterfowl calls, including 17 duck calls. Calls range from the Timberhole duck call, an easy-blowing, high-pitched call that makes the throaty hen rasp at the low end of the scale and is perfect for flooded timber hunting, to the metal-reed duck call and an acrylic model. Thirteen goose call models are available including the classic Presentation Goose Call, several regular goose calls, three flute type including the A-50 Canadian Honker, the original "flute" Canada goose call. Also available are a snow and blue goose and a specklebelly model. The Sonderman 66 Duck Call is proudly named after Olt's master call maker, Al Sonderman. It's an easy-to-blow call with great tone and volume. The Olt D-2 OSCD Duck Call is a cut-down, shortened version of the popular keyhole-style duck call that can be blown loud for open water or soft for flooded timber and small potholes. The D-2 is made of Cycolac and does not absorb moisture. The Millennium Magnum Duck Call is a molded waterproof Cycolac call with a double reed that produces a high-pitched, raspy sound. Olt also has two calls, a double- and a triple-reed model, made of American walnut. Both can be used to create loud calls for open water, or can be used for softer, closer-in calls.

Sure-Shot Game Calls manufactures the Yentzen World Champion Duck Calls with their patented double reed. They also carry a wide range of other wooden duck and wooden and plastic goose calls. Their Imperial line includes the Imperial Champion Double Reed Duck, Imperial Honker Goose, Imperial Snow Goose, and Imperial Speckle Belly Goose Calls.

The Duck Commander calls include the Brown Sugar, a soft and sweet, easy-blowing call for hunting timber and close-in work; the Black Pepper, a super-loud, hot tone that's great for open water and flooded fields; Original Duck Commander Call, redesigned with an improved look and better sound; Cutdown Reacher Call with a flat, raspy sound that's a great timber call for the advanced caller; and the Mallard Drake Call, built especially to lure call-shy, late-season mallards. The Goose Commander Call Speck-1 is built for "goose-aholics" with the famous Phil Robertson sound. The call is pre-bored for exact breath pressure, and has removable end cap for soft or loud volume control.

Faulk's, one of the oldest waterfowl call companies, carries a full line of duck and goose calls. Many of the calls are made of select hardwoods such as zebrawood.

The Mallardtone Mallard Mag is a double-reed call with a loud, raspy sound that is especially designed for the aggressive hunter. Also available is the

Diver calls, such as the Mallardtone shown, are used to produce the purrs of bluebills, canvasbacks, and other divers.

Timber Mag, a double-reed ABS plastic call that provides a more mellow, raspy sound. Their Diver Mag deceives all types of diver ducks, canvasbacks, bluebills, redheads, ringnecks, or goldeneyes.

The Iverson Super Standard call was developed as an all-around call that uses a flat platform and curved single-reed design, making it very easy to use. It's great for open-field and distance calling. Their Super Timber Call has a shorter barrel, giving it a rich, natural rasp and high register that is perfect for timber and close-in calling.

Three of the most unusual types of calls I've tested are the Flex Tone calls from Wiley Duck. They have an acrylic reed assembly (mimicking a duck's larynx of hard tissue) and a flexible barrel (simulating the duck's neck and tongue or soft tissue). The patented call with its flexible barrel molds to your lips, is durable, and won't break. You can change the sound of the call simply by how you squeeze the barrel. The calls are available in a Double Reed Mallard Call with an Arkansas sound for flooded timber; Single Reed Mallard Call for loud ringing hail calls; and the Black Mallard Call, an excellent call for the beginner.

The Southern Game Calls' molded Little Joe comes in a variety of colors plus signature colors. It is a replica of their handmade acrylic calls and is complemented by a brass band and hand-cut reeds. The Greenhead is a beginner's best call. It features an unconventional double reed with a cocobolo barrel dressed with a brass band and a polyacrylic stopper. The reeds are designed to do a ringing hail call and come down to raspy quacks. The Nasty Boy is designed for timber and marsh hunting and features a pressurized system that allows you to sound like many different ducks—from the high-pitched to the low raspy tones.

Cutt Down Game Calls, "Arkansas Style" Single Reed acrylic calls, available in Timber and Competition models, are precision cut on a CNC mill, not a jig, then hand tuned by David Wiegand and Marcus Keith. Also available are their Brass Banded Acrylic "Cajun Style" Timber Mallard Calls with double-locking O-rings to ensure an airtight fit and to prevent loss of call components. The Cocobolo Green Timber/Cajun Hen Call duplicates the sounds of a mallard hen with a craw full of rice, acorns, and so forth, very nasal and scratchy. Cutt Down's entire line of duck and goose calls are available in Advantage Wetlands camo. Cutt Down Game Calls offer a big sound in a small package. Some of their duck calls are only 3 inches long but incredibly loud. The timber series adds rasp to the volume for hunting in river bottoms, swamps, and green timber. Also offered is a less expensive line of calls built entirely of "Silicon Injection Molded Polycarbonate Plastic." They are easy to blow because there isn't a large barrel to fill with air before the reed starts to vibrate. With the reeds close to the mouth, little air pressure is needed and correct back pressure is easy to maintain. Cutt Down reed system is now available in both "Cajun-style" double reed, and an Arkansas-style single-reed call in competition and timber hunting models.

The Foiles Migrators "Strait Meat" Mallard Call is available as a single-reed call; double-reed calls are available on request. The call is extra loud for those high migrators and for big, open water, or for the toughest calling contests. The Strait Meat Mallard can also be used soft and raspy for flooded corn-fields or timber and is crafted from acrylic and/or classic wood.

Bay Area Products Inc., makers of Fowl Foolers Waterfowl Calls and Decoys, has a full line of custom calls. The Flooded Timber Call has the unique ability to climb the musical scale from top to bottom without losing raspiness. The Arky is a loud, single-reed Arkansas-style call designed for loud blowing, attention-getting hail calls. The Cajun is a soft Louisiana Cajun-style call that

Shaker calls, such as the Quaker Boy shown, can be used to easily create the feed chatter of ducks simply by shaking.

has a soft quack and blows easily for a double-reed call. The Gullet is perhaps the most unique custom call, producing a squeaky quack like a mallard with a craw full of grain and is designed for flooded field hunting over crops such as corn, rice, and wheat. All custom calls are made of walnut, but are available in other species. Also available is an array of calls for whistling ducks and six different goose calls.

The Knight & Hale Double Reed Acrylic Duck Call makes all duck sounds easily. The molded-acrylic call features two reeds—excellent for close-in calling and for coaxing ducks into flooded timber. Other great calls from this well-known company include their Single Reed Acrylic (amber mist) Duck Call, which is very effective for open-water conditions when calls must be heard a long distance. Also available is a full line of Canada and snow goose calls.

A number of duck calls are available from Quaker Boy, including the Easy Chuckle shaker call. Now anyone can make feed chuckles simply by

Goose calls come in a variety of sizes, shapes, and styles.

shaking their hand. Also included is the Woody Wood Duck Whistle, which accurately reproduces the calls of woodies. The Quaker Boy Camo Quack Master, available in Advantage Wetlands, is easy to handle and call in any weather and has a durable single-reed construction for open water. The Camo Raspy Quack Master is a double-reed construction for producing raspy sounds to call-shy birds in timber. The Quaker Boy Acrylic Pro Hunter's Duck Call Series adds hardness to the sound due to the material and is available in both single- and double-reed construction. If you prefer to customize your duck calls, their Duck Call Reed Package includes: two single reeds, two sets of double reeds, two rubber stoppers, and two cork stoppers. Although made for Quaker Boy Duck Calls, the reed package can be used with most other calls. The Shorty Hybrid Goose Flute uses an acrylic barrel short-type, blow-operated call, with a short reed, to provide the sound of a flute call. The Wingmaster operates like an old blow-type call, but has the sound of a modern-day flute call. The Long Neck Goose Flute, like most flute-type goose calls, requires achieving back pressure by cupping your hands over the end of the call.

The flute call is the easiest to blow, especially for beginners, as expert caller David Bilman of Lohman demonstrates.

Woods Wise has a number of waterfowl calls including their Classic Snow Goose with a removable plug to automatically control back pressure; the Classic Mallard, a single-reed design that's easy to blow; and the Classic Goose that features an easy-to-blow, "long-reed" design. All feature a weatherproof, hard plastic body. Realtree Hardwoods 20/200 Calls are available for an additional cost.

From Penn's Woods comes their "Saucey Hen" duck call. Made from high-density plastics, the call produces the full range of duck vocalizations. Each call is individually tuned and sanitized by Penn's Woods duck calling professionals and comes with a camo lanyard. The Penn's Woods "Committer" Goose is a short-reed call. Made from select, custom-turned hardwood, each call comes with camo lanyard and is hand tuned.

PRO TIPS

"I think a man should look for a duck call that he can blow, not what his buddy blows," said Harold Knight. "I blow single- and double-reed calls and I like both of them. I don't think blowing a single type of duck call will work. Somebody told me one time that if you sound like a duck it will work anyplace, and it will to a certain extent, but lots of times you need a high-pitched sound, and at other times you're hunting a place where you need a lower sound so that you don't blow them out. The acoustics are so different in the different places you hunt, woods versus big open fields, windy days, north winds, and things like that. You need at least two calls that are tuned differently. It's like turkey hunting; most people don't go turkey hunting with one call, and you shouldn't go duck hunting with one call."

"I recommend for someone who hasn't done much calling to pick a call that is easy to blow," said Kelly Haydel. "A lot of calls require a lot of air, some calls require a lot of grunting into the call, and if you're a person who hasn't done a lot of calling, it could take a lot of time to build up a technique to do it and also to build up the wind required. A lot of the double-reed calls out on the market these days don't require as much grunting into the call, and they also don't require as much air to produce the correct sound."

Quality lanyards are necessary to hold a variety of calls and prevent dropping them in the mud or water.

COMPETITION CALLS

"Competition callers look for the more versatile calls," said goose and duck call competition winner Brad Harris. "The pro series calls, the calls that have a flat sounding board. In other words, the flatter the sounding board, the more control you have to have on the call, but the more range, full range in tone you have. It will have the long-range, high-end hail call, loud, yet the call will reverse back to very, very soft quacks and feed calls. So it is a full-range call you're looking for to produce that calling pattern that competition calling requires. Many standard calls that you kill ducks with may not be suited for competition because they are not considered a full-range call."

3

CALLING DUCKS

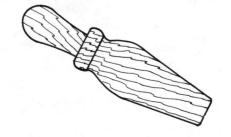

At first they're mere specks in the distance. You place the call to your lips and blow a loud, long, pleading hail call. Expectantly you watch the flight of mallards, and your heart really begins to pound as you see the dozen or so birds swing around low over the line of trees and head your way. Another call, this time shorter and more demanding; then you stop calling. It's the last few days of the season and the big, red-legged birds are extremely wary. In fact, they're call-shy. You've already worked four flights, got one flight in, and took a couple of greenheads. You desperately want this flight. It's a tough morning, no wind, and the decoys have a skim of ice that you have worked hard to keep open.

The flock comes straight in, then wheels just out of gun range at the last minute and starts away from you. You desperately throw out a come-back call. It appears they will keep going away from you, then they turn back and start a long swing behind the blind. You give feed chatter mixed in with a few raspy old hen quacks and hear an answering quack from an old Susy in the flock.

You too can learn to call ducks. A duck call is basically a reed musical instrument. Take your time to learn the basics, then simply practice.

You smile to yourself. They make a slow turn over the decoys, then disappear behind the blind again. You don't move a muscle but continue the low chatter and mix in soft quacks. You desperately want to look behind the blind for the birds, but everyone in the blind stays statue still. Then there is another soft quack just above, and you know if you had moved you would have lost the birds. Out of the corner of your eye you see the flight start to turn away again, and this time you give a short, fast, demanding sit-down call—and they immediately wheel back. It's another agonizing minute that seems like an eternity until you finally see big, red, waving feet above your set and then they're in the decoys. "Now" you shout to your companions and within seconds, four greenheads float on the icy water. You beam with happiness as the dog begins to retrieve and your companions pound you on the back and compliment you on your calling.

You can learn to calls ducks. It's fun, easy, and adds immense pleasure to your duck hunting. In fact, anyone can learn to blow a duck call if they take their time, learn the basics first, then simply spend time practicing. The first and best way to learn duck calling is from an expert caller who will take the time to teach you the skills. Unfortunately experts who will share their secrets are rare. Many good callers would prefer to keep their techniques to themselves. Another method, and one that is easier for beginners, is to listen to one of the calling cassettes or CDs on the market and/or watch calling videos available from the various call manufacturers. You can also learn the basics from this book chapter. Hearing the various sounds, whether from a tape or in the field, however, is invaluable. One great way is to visit marshes and waterfowl refuges during the spring migration and use a cassette tape recorder to record the various sounds. Although several different types of calls are available, as described in the previous chapter, and also different sounds from the different species and even the different sexes, the calls of the hen mallard are the most common and will attract most other ducks.

HOLDING THE CALL

The first step is to learn to grasp the call properly. Encircle the front or small end of the call with your thumb and forefinger. Cup your fingers around the end of the call to form a sort of "bell." You can control the tone of the call as well as the volume by opening and closing your fingers.

Holding the call properly is important. Grasp the front end of the barrel with your thumb and forefinger, using the remaining fingers to create a "bell."

The next step is to place the bottom edge of the call on top of your bottom lip. Bring the top edge of the call against your top lip and close your lips tightly so no air can escape around the call.

BREATH CONTROL

Controlling your breath is the most important factor in making real "duck" sounds, rather than the nasal quacks often given by beginners. Most duck calls are not blown into like a whistle, although you can get by with some

Place the bottom edge of the call on top of your bottom lip. Then tilt the top edge of the call up against your top lip. Close your lips to prevent air from escaping around the call.

double-reed calls. Blowing into the call usually produces a hollow, unrealistic sound. Instead, most duck calls are "grunted" or "growled" into. Bring air up from your chest by rolling your diaphragm upward and forcing air through the call. This is the hardest part of learning how to use a duck call, but it is very important. To help learn the technique, hold your breath and try to exhale at the same time. You will feel your diaphragm roll upward with the effort. Done correctly, with the call in place, this will produce an audible "grunt" along with the sound made by the call.

Most duck calls are grunted or growled into to produce the "ducky" sounds. This is done by rolling your diaphragm upward, producing an audible grunt.

You must also say a "word" sound at the same time you force air through the call. Although there are a number of different word sounds that can be used, three words will produce the sounds needed for most duck calls. They are WICK, TICK-IT, and KAK. Some callers like to use the word QUACK instead of WICK.

WICK or QUACK is used to make the quacking sounds of both the hen and drake mallard, as well as most other puddle ducks. Say the word WICK and at the same time grunt through the call. Take your time learning this basic sound. Then learn to stretch it out, to WI— CK, which adds more realism to the sound. Practice making the sound loud, moderate, and soft sounding. If you learn to make just this one call, you can call ducks. Simply issue the single sound fairly softly when ducks are overhead or circling the decoys. The call should be given contentedly, like a hen mallard that is comfortable, feeding or loafing.

Once you've mastered the single word, string it into a five-time sequence. WI-CK, WI-CK, WI-CK, WI-CK, WI-CK. The call should be fairly soft, sounding like the quack, quack, quack, quack, quack of a lone hen mallard.

The next word to learn is TICK-IT. This produces the soft feeding chatter of mallards and puddle ducks when pronounced into the call. Say the word TICK-IT and, at the same time, move your tongue up and down, bouncing your tongue off the roof of your mouth. Start saying the word slowly, then increase the tempo until you run the words together. The sound should be TICK-IT, TICK-IT, TICK-IT, TICK-IT-TICK-IT-TICK-IT-TICK-IT-TICK-IT-TICK-IT-TICK-IT.

Don't get discouraged trying to learn this sound. It's the hardest sound to make, but is extremely effective when ducks are circling your blind. It's a good

You must also say word sounds at the same time you "grunt" into the call. Different word sounds are used for the different call sounds.

Most ducks will respond to the quack and feeding sounds of mallards.

idea for one hunter in the blind to continue making this call while other callers make other sounds. Shaker-type feeding chuckle calls on the market make it easy to reproduce the feeding sounds simply by shaking the call. The basic patterns are the same, and you can shake the shaker calls to produce the feeding sounds while you use mouth calls to produce the other sounds, but it's pretty busy stuff.

Alternating single quacks with the feed chuckle is an extremely effective tactic to entice ducks that are close in but wary or call-shy. Keep the calls fairly slow, soft, and contented sounding.

The word KAK is used to create the cluck made by a hen mallard. Say the word KAK at the same time you grunt through the call. Once you learn to make the sound, mix it in with the feed chatter for another effective close-in call. This can also be used in conjunction with the soft quacks. A good rhythm might consist of TICK-IT-TICK-IT-TICK-IT . . . KAK, KAK, KAK . . . TICK-IT-TICK-IT-TICK-IT-TICK-IT . . . WI—CK . . . TICK-IT-TICK-IT-TICK-IT-TICK-IT . . . KAK, KAK, KAK . . . TICK-IT-TICK-IT-TICK-IT-TICK-IT-TICK-IT . . . WI—CK.

Granted, you won't be able to make the sounds perfectly at first. Just keep practicing making all these sounds until you are comfortable with them and can produce them easily. Don't hurry to the next step until you're comfortable with producing the individual sounds.

Then you can use the various sounds to produce a variety of calling patterns that suit the various hunting situations. Duck calls are produced in rhythms or patterns, and the timing or pattern is as important as the individual sounds. Six basic calling patterns can be used, although the actual calling patterns vary somewhat across the country. For instance, timber callers in the South produce quite a bit different type of sound and pattern from the open-lake hunters of the upper Midwest.

The basic patterns, consist of: hail or highball, close-in hail call, comeback, close-in confidence, lonesome hen, and feeding chatter.

HAIL CALL

When ducks are at a distance, the hail or highball call is used to attract their attention. This is a popular call in open water, field, or marsh, but rarely used in close-in timber or small pothole hunting. The distance it will attract ducks varies according to wind and weather, as well as other factors such as existing vegetation. Under the right conditions, in open country, a good hail call can attract ducks a half mile away. It can also flare call-shy ducks.

To produce the hail call, say the word WICK as loud as you can into the call, forcing enough air through the call so the sound will break on a high note. Don't produce a squealing sound, but a loud, high-pitched quack. This takes a great deal of effort, especially when first learning to call. Once you learn to make the sound break to the high note, then learn to hold the high sound for the count of five. Once you learn to create the high note and hold it for the count of five, or a couple of seconds, then go up to the high note, and say the word WICK five times, holding each a second or two. Then come down the scale fast, repeating the word WICK four or five times.

The pattern is WI . . . CK, WI . . . CK. W . . . CK, WI . . . CK, WI . . . CK-WICK-WICK-WICK-WICK. This call takes a great deal of practice and time for most beginners to learn, so don't give up.

Once you learn to make the individual sounds, the next step is to put the sounds into a calling pattern. Several different patterns are used for different situations.

CLOSE-IN HAIL CALL

A shorter version of the hail call is used when ducks are closer and is called the close-in hail call. This is also sometimes called the five-quack landing call. It is made by saying the word WICK in five short, fast quacks. Start high, then come down fast. Stretching out the first quack can also be effective at times. The close-in hail call is not quite as loud as the highball and is used when ducks are 50 to 100 yards out and warily circling. When the flock turns and starts toward you, go into a feed chatter mixed with clucks or individual soft quacks until the birds are in the decoys or fly into shooting range. When hunting public land or there is a lot of competition from other hunters, sometimes giving the close-in hail call over and over again will attract the attention of passing ducks.

COME-BACK CALL

If ducks begin to come toward you, then turn away, give the come-back call. The come-back call is similar to the close-in hail call, with some differences. The word WICK is used three times fairly high, but not as loud as the hail call, then WICK is said while coming down the scale very fast. At the end add three or four more WICKs, getting slower with each, then drag out the last wick with a begging sound on the end. WICK-WICK-WICK, WICK WICK WICK WICK . . . WI . . . CK, WI . . . CK, WI . . . . . . CK. This is an extremely effective call for ducks that may be undecided about coming into your decoys. The come-back call is also good when ducks are trying to land just outside your decoys. If the ducks turn and go away from you, blow the come-back call over and over until the ducks turn toward you. Leave out the begging sound on the end until the ducks turn back. Try to sound demanding on the first part of the call, but beg on the end. When ducks turn and start toward you, go into the close-in call.

CLOSE-IN CALL

Say the word WICK but drag it out: WI . . . . . . CK. At the same time come down the scale in a slow, drawn-out sound.

The close-in call is more drawn out and with a begging sound. Stretch out the word WICK as long as possible with each sound. Use the word three or four times in a series. WI . . . CK . . . WI . . . CK . . . WI . . . CK . . . WI . . . CK. Anyone who can use the close-in call, and mixed in with feed chuckles, can call ducks anyplace, often more effectively than a loud caller. This is a favorite with timber callers or for those areas where ducks can't be seen long distances, and quite often simply appear overhead.

LONESOME HEN

This is one of my favorite calls. I quite often use it throughout the hunt, even when I can't see ducks. Even if nothing is happening, about every 30 minutes or so I give the lonesome hen call. The lonesome hen is a soft, raspy series of quacks made using the word WICK and adding in the word KAK to produce the cluck as well as feed chatter for an extremely effective close-in call for wary mallards. WI . . . CK-KAK-KAK-KAK-WI . . . CK-WI . . . CK. Throw in a little feed chatter as well and you'll have a good chance at even call-wary mallards.

DRAKE MALLARD SOUNDS

The drake call is a confidence sound. When you throw in the drake whistle, it is exactly what the ducks are hearing—that old hen quacking and feed chatter—but drakes also give little whistly, buzzy-type soft quacks. It is a confidence sound, a great call to hunt with. Primarily the drake call is a close-in call.

OTHER DUCK SOUNDS

Although all puddle ducks and most divers will respond to the basic sounds and patterns described for mallards, specialty calls can increase your success with some species of ducks. Teal, pintail, widgeon, and wood ducks also make whistling or tittering sounds. Adding in those sounds can add to

Whistle calls used for pintails, teal, wood ducks, and other birds can be added into the pattern. Terry Shaughnessy of Hackberry Rod and Gun Club in Louisiana uses them with mallard quacks and patterns.

your calling pattern. You can use a simple plastic "policeman's" whistle or any number of special whistle calls made just for calling these ducks. The whistle calls are usually blown fairly softly and are mixed in with soft quacks made with a regular mallard call. You can make the pattern twice as effective with two callers, one providing the normal mallard sounds while another does the whistles and titters.

DIVER CALLS

Divers are very, very coarse in their quacks without a lot of high-pitched sounds. Divers almost have a purring buzz to their quack, a distinctly different quack than puddle ducks. The quacks of diving ducks are usually more guttural and sharper, almost like the barking of a small dog. Divers also produce growls and purrs.

You work the ducks the same way, but the quacks are more exaggerated and aggressive. Use long-range-type calls to get their attention and then work

Diver calls are used to make the growls and purrs as well as the sharp, doglike barking sound of divers. The calling patterns are similar to mallards, but start out high, drop fast, and end up with the growls.

them the same way when you get them in close. Back down on the volume and do a lot more coaxing.

A number of diving duck calls are on the market, although you can produce the sharp quacking with a high-pitched mallard call. You can also make the rasping burrrrr sound on a mallard call by fluttering your tongue against the roof of your mouth as you grunt into the call.

Using a call made especially for diving ducks is best because diver calls are usually fairly fast. The pattern starts out high and fast and drops quickly as the birds approach, ending in a raspy, low-pitched series of growls and purrs.

GADWALL CALLS

"Several years ago the population of gadwalls really exploded," said Kelly Haydel. "A lot of hunters looking to extend their hunting day and to fill out their bag limit wanted every advantage they could have. We then came out with the gadwall call to produce the nasally type little quacks that the gadwall make, and it can be really effective. When gadwall start congregating and bunching up in an area, they talk back and forth to each other with a soft TAT TAT TAT TAT sound. Hunters should first get the birds' attention with a single mallard hail call, then take the gadwall call and do the soft TAT TAT TAT TAT sounds that give a realistic scenario of how the bird sounds in the wild. Basically it is the same as calling pintails: You get their attention with a mallard call, then switch over to the pintail whistle as a confidence call."

PRO TIPS

"The experienced waterfowler learns to watch the flight of ducks, noting how they move, and learns to listen to them," said my son, and longtime waterfowl guide, Mark Burch. "Note how they move and pitch in the air currents and change your calls to bring them in. Listen to how the ducks are talking to you. If the lead hen is doing a lot of gabbling and a lot of quacks, then the calling you throw back should be similar to their flight talk. In the beginning of the season, when the calling is fresh, a lot of highball calling mixed up with fancy calling is often used on the big reservoirs I normally hunt. There's a tremendous amount of competition, and quite often the best callers are the ones who get the birds. As the season wears on, however, hunting pressure increases, and the birds become call-shy from all the overcalling of inexperienced hunters. Then you need to learn when to be loud and when to be quiet. Use loud calling on windy days, soft calling on calm days."

"It's important to watch and listen to the birds," says waterfowl guide Mark Burch. "Follow their lead. If the lead hen is doing a lot of calling, you should mimic her."

"It takes a right smart amount of practice to be an accomplished duck caller," said David Hale of Knight & Hale. "You don't have to be a contest winner to call ducks, but you do basically need to know how to make a good come-back call and a good greeting call. Those are the two most important calls you'll make when duck hunting. The feeding call is another call that's sometimes used, although it's for close-in calling. For the most part, you really don't need to get into all the contest-type stuff, the long, high-sounding highballs or hail calls, especially when first starting to call ducks.

"When duck calling it's best for those hunting in a blind together to learn to call in unison. They also need to be able to read the ducks; one caller really doesn't need to be screaming out while the other is feed calling. The excellent callers I've hunted with tend to play off each other, and basically call the same way. It's kind of like a good quartet harmonizing together. I would pick the best one or two callers in the blind and let them do the calling, because I personally feel like you're sometimes throwing in too many different sounds that are out of kilter if everybody is out there blowing a duck call."

"Anybody can make a duck call sound, but you also have to know when not to call," said Tom Matthews, president of Avery Outdoors, manufacturer of waterfowling equipment, and longtime waterfowler. I've hunted with Tom numerous times and noted he has a very distinct calling pattern. "We have several rules with our callers," Tom explained. "When ducks are directly over you, doesn't matter whether they're low or high, you just don't call, make a sound, or whatever. They can look straight down and see something is wrong."

Like Mark, Tom primarily hunts public land—his favorite two places are in the Mississippi Delta and along the White River in Arkansas—and he finds the calling techniques vary with each. One is a big cypress swamp. "There's not an ounce of food on it," Tom said. "The ducks don't come in for food, they're coming from the surrounding soybeans and rice fields to rest. These are always big flights of cautious ducks. Anything breeding or going to food is easier to kill than something that is just looking for a place to sit down and rest, because there's a lot of choices to sit down. It is public waterfowling, and the best duck callers in the world are down there. You've got them 300 yards away on one side and 100 yards away on the other side and they've all got 48 decoys or so out. These aren't very big holes or openings in the swamp. We're also hunting out of boat blinds because there aren't any permanent structures. We first hit the ducks hard with a highball call, not the contest type, or the kind you hear up around Reelfoot Lake, but shorter and more 'ducky' sounding. Then we quickly change to a softer, shorter come-back or sit-down-type call. These ducks are always workable because they're flying over at a workable height, but you really have to compete for them.

"Another public area we hunt is totally different. It's a great green-timber food area with lots of acorns. When they come over, they're a lot closer, generally right over the trees, already looking for a place to come in. In this case the first call is almost always a greeting or come-back-type call, hardly ever a highball. It's more of a staccato-type call. Then we may do some feed calls. I think a lot of people overdo feed calling just because it's something they feel comfortable doing, but I don't think you generally hear ducks feed calling a lot.

"The third place we hunt is right by the Mississippi River. Ducks are coming from the fields, coming to rest, and they have lots of lakes with huge open waters to sit down in. We have to hide our boat blinds right up against the willows along the bank, and it's hard to convince the ducks to land within 20 yards of a line of trees when they can land right out in the center of the water. So in that place we stay on the calls hard-hard-hard. On one hunt with David Hale and Harold Knight we had four mallards that had committed totally to our decoys, but we had been having trouble having the ducks come on in. Harold, I, and my two business partners, Tate and Allen, stayed on them real hard while David filmed and they literally lit 15 feet from the boat. You really have to learn to adapt your calling to each situation and actually to each day."

"A beginning caller should not feel intimidated by veteran callers," said Kelly Haydel of Haydel's Calls. "Sounding natural is really the key. A lot of callers like to show off and they are really calling in more of a contest calling style with 15, 20, or 30 notes in a hail call. A live duck, a natural duck does not do that. If at all possible, hear the birds in the wild. Go where you can listen to the birds and hear what they are doing and imitate the natural bird. Watch the birds; how many notes do they make? You've got birds sitting on the water calling to birds in the air; how do the birds respond? That's one of the benefits of being down here in Louisiana and being in the marsh so much—I'm around it all the time and I see these birds and how they react. Usually about seven or maybe nine notes on a hail call is enough to get the bird's attention. Typically I try to stick with about five notes with most of my calling. I can change how I sound on that call just by the rhythm and the tempo, still using just five notes. I can do a standard greeting call where all five notes are all about the same

Loud demanding calls are used to get the attention of distant ducks, especially on open water and large marshes.

length and about the same intensity. I can then take those same five notes, and stretch the first note out longer to create what is called a pleading call. I can take those same five notes, shorten them, speed up my rhythm, make them a little more choppy, and I've created an excited come-back call. So with the five notes, I've got the three different rhythms, and with that I can do just about every scenario I need."

"I've found that most times timber is a place where ducks like to come when they are through feeding and want to rest," said Harold Knight. "I like to give some quick quacking series, like *quack, quack, quack*. You know, you give a series like the ducks are content and in that timber sort of resting and happy. I don't give a whole lot of feeding calls in timber. I also found out that if I can get some kind of movement out of my decoys in that timber it really makes a difference. Sometimes I just use my boot to make a ripple and some low sound. Now if I'm hunting open fields or open water on days when the wind is blowing, then I want a high-pitched call where the sound will really get his attention. If the ducks start working in, then I just change calls to a double reed when they get closer. But I like a single-reed call, something that will really call a long distance.

"You can blow ducks out coming in close. I don't like to blow to ducks or geese when they are directly over my head. I like to watch them. I like to see them balled up and come out of the clear skies on those northern days in cold, clear weather. But, when they come in and make a circle, I like to blow real fast to them when they've got their back end to me. Like *quack, quack, quack*, and turn them around. Then I start slowing down and give some feed calling and then some softer calls when they get in close. There are so many verbals in duck and goose calling, and lots to take into consideration. Where you hunt, whether you're close to a reservation; the time of year, late season versus early season; everything will change your calling pattern on ducks and geese. Ducks are hunted in Canada and all the way south. I think the farther south they are, the more educated they are. I think the migratory ducks and geese that are left are a lot more educated when they get real far south."

"First and foremost is knowing when to blow the call," said Jarad Perkins, winner of the 1999 and 2000 Winchester Open World, as well as numerous other championships. Jarad is also a duck and goose guide for Avery Outdoors in Arkansas and hunts across the continent from the North to Mexico. "It's more important to know when to blow the call than knowing how to blow a duck call. A lot of people know how to blow a duck call pretty good, but

"Closer, more begging sounds are used in timber hunting," says Larry Cleghorn of Wildlife Farms in Arkansas. These sounds are also used when the ducks are close in but not yet committed to the dekes.

I'm not so much worried about how good you sound as knowing when to do what. Of course, it helps if you sound good on it too, but I'd rather sound worse and know when to blow.

"One way to learn is being around people who know when to call, then use trial and error. No two groups of ducks are going to respond the same to calls. They might on certain days; for instance, if one bunch likes less calls, then probably the other ones will like less calling too. You're not, however, going to be able to learn everything from somebody else. You're going to have to learn some on your own by watching what the birds do and being able to read the birds when they are flying and how they are working and how they are reacting to what you're doing."

"A lot of people get away from actual realism, get away from what ducks actually sound like," said Kelly Powers, goose competition winner, Avery pro staffer, and waterfowl guide with Final Flight Outfitters in Tennessee. "People listen more to people than going to see what actual ducks sound like. As far as people teaching others, they can help shorten the process of learning to call, but the best teachers are actually the birds you are trying to imitate. I suggest you just go listen to live birds on the water and see their reactions under different conditions, the different things they do according to the weather or whatever. For example, in cold-weather conditions, ducks or geese are going to do different things than in warm-weather conditions. If you're watching a pond, lake, flooded field, refuge, or whatever, 300 yards out is a bunch of ducks sitting there. If they get up, fly 200 yards, and sit down at another location, you should think to yourself, why did they leave. When they are in flight, you should ask, how are they going to land, are they going to land over here, or why did they land there, is there a different food source or maybe other birds are there."

"I grew up on green-timber hunting," said Will Primos of Primos Hunting Calls. "A lot of people haven't had a chance to experience that because there's not much green timber north of Arkansas, but it's really neat to bring mallards down into the timber potholes. One of the major things to do, when you've got your decoys all around you and you're hugging a tree, is just kick the water with your foot and make a lot of ripples and commotion. Any kind of water movement you can create while hunting the pin oak flats for mallards is always good. Of course you have to have workable ducks; you've got your flight ducks and you've got your working ducks. You don't want to call too loud. My favorite call for that situation is our Wench Double Reed Call. But I do a bit of modification to it, extending the bottom reed about ½ inch out past the top reed. This tends to give me a little more control, especially when I'm working ducks and they're coming in and really looking hard. What is neat is to have two or three good callers who can complement each other and sound like a bunch of ducks on the water. Which is exactly what ducks are looking for—large concentrations of other ducks to come to."

CONTEST CALLING

"You can get by with some imperfections in calling when you're hunting, if you have a good decoy spread and a good place to hunt," said contest call winner Brad Harris. "On stage they are looking for perfection. You have to really have your call down pat, have your control down pat. You need a call that is full range, be able to hit everything from a 50-count hail call in some instances, and then run your call through the come-backs, the five quacks, and the drake sounds and also have a good feed chatter. You must have a routine that is flawless, no squeaks, no short calls, things that would be considered imperfect. You can kill all the ducks you want in good areas if you've got the basic quacks down, five quacks or the basic ducky sounds; you can be very successful in the marsh but it wouldn't help you on the contest side because you would need to be a full-range caller who blows a very perfect pattern.

"A typical pattern is starting out calling for long-range ducks with a series of hail calls, depending on the competition you're in. Some, such as Stuttgart, are looking for 50-note hail calls. If you run three series of those types of hail calls, you'd better have some air. Generally you start out hailing the ducks, getting their attention long range, then in your mind visualize the ducks turning and coming to you so you would cut back and do more coaxing the ducks as they come in. Do a lot of five quacks and single quacks and some feed stuff as you coax the ducks in, then visualize the ducks circling and leaving and so you get on a series of come-back calls, making them turn back around and come back. Then you work the ducks again with five quacks, single quacks, feed calls fairly aggressively, and then as the ducks lock their wings, you go into coaxing them, wanting them to land, and that is softer sounds, soft quacks, soft feed calls. You're actually putting the ducks down on the water. Basically in competition you are hailing them, bringing

Duck calls sound much better if you clean them regularly.

them in, then when they leave, you make them come back and then you coax them in to land."

"Pick out a good call," said Jarad Perkins. "One that works for you. Don't pay any attention to the name on the call. Just pick out a call that fits you the best and stick with it. Don't jump around to a bunch of different calls. And then just practice. Videoing yourself is the best way to practice. Video yourself, go to big contests and video everybody else, then watch and learn how they are doing it and compare your video to that."

MAINTENANCE AND TUNING OF CALLS

"Maintenance is just basically keeping your calls clean, especially inside where the reed is located. When your call starts to make a funky sound, it's probably gummed up with saliva or seeds or whatever you've dropped it in," says Brad Harris. While I'm in the field I usually don't want to take a call apart, but I'll take the guts out of the barrel and use a dollar bill, anything flat, to slide under the reed and saw it back and forth to clean the call.

Then when I get home and I want to do a major cleaning, I dismantle the call and wash the reed, clean the insert and wedges and get all the debris and stains off, and then reassemble the call. The key is to try to keep them clean. I don't like to throw them up on the dash of the truck and let the sun bake them. You want to keep them out of direct sunlight for the most part and clean them up before you store them away for the end of the year so they will be fresh and ready to go for the following year.

"Tuning calls is something you want to be careful with. All calls come out of the factory tuned and ready to perform to certain specifications, but as hunters get proficient on their calls they want to hear a little bit different sounds and create different sounds, and so they manipulate the reeds. The reeds are generally made of Mylar or some Mylar-type material. The ends of those reeds can be sanded lightly with fine sandpaper to thin them out so they will respond quicker, become a little higher pitched. You can pull the reed out to lengthen it, but anytime you change or alter a duck or goose call reed even a couple of thousandths of an inch, you're going to change the tone completely. So if you're tuning your call, you want to take it off minutely and blow the call every time you make an alteration. You don't want to take a lot off, whether you're lengthening it by pulling the reed out or taking a pair of scissors and cutting the reed off, just ever so slightly, and unless you know what you're doing you're going to ruin a few calls, or at least ruin a few reeds until you get it down pat. You can feather those calls, take some of the thickness off the ends; you can lengthen them, you can shorten them. Every little thing you do is going to change that call, and you want to do everything in very minute steps until you know what you're doing."

4

CALLING GEESE

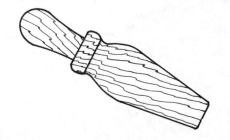

We heard them well before we saw them. Loud *ker-honks* were echoing off the early-morning-calm water of Truman Reservoir. My oldest son, Mark, and I were out of the blind arranging decoys when we heard the first sounds and just had time to get to the side of the blind before the big birds topped a slight rise 100 yards or so from our blind. Their flight direction was almost directly across in front of us, but Mark gave a series of fast K-LUKs. His calls, combined with the four dozen floating Canada decoys, turned the flock of 50 or so geese our direction. If you don't get excited when Canada geese are coming into your decoys, it's time to check with your local mortician. This was no exception. Although the big birds were slowly winging directly at us, it seemed like time stood still. My heart was pounding much faster than the slow steady wingbeats of the oncoming birds, and it seemed to take forever for the birds to cross the quarter-mile stretch. With geese there is always doubt. Will they come in, circle, or perhaps flare at the last minute? Canada geese are never a given. Mark was giving an occasional K-LUK while I chuckled background feed

Calling geese to the decoys is extremely exciting and also easily learned. In many ways goose calling is more forgiving and easier to learn than duck calling.

gabble. Out of the corner of my eye I saw Mark's knees shaking from excitement. Then the birds passed the outer edge of the decoys and were within range, but I didn't give the order to shoot. They were still coming and Mark and I, both entranced, watched the entire flock begin to settle down in the decoys, the nearest birds less than 20 yards away. It was easy. We collected Christmas dinner in a hurry, then spent the remainder of the morning calling in flock after flock just to watch them come into the decoys.

Calling Canada geese into decoys is rarely that easy. In fact, I've more than paid for that one day with many frustrating hours spent working super-wary birds. Although bringing the wary birds into the decoys can be tough, just about anyone can learn to blow a goose call in a matter of days using the steps shown in this chapter. As with duck calling, it's a matter of practice. The more you work at it, the better you'll become. We begin with Canada goose calls because all other geese will respond to those sounds; then we'll cover the other geese—specklebellies, snows, and blues.

The sounds and words also vary depending on whether you're using a traditional, flute type, or the popular short-reed goose call.

TRADITIONAL GOOSE CALLS

Learning to hold the call properly is the first step. Grasp the front tube of the call between your thumb and forefinger. The volume and tone can be varied by opening and closing your fingers. Opening your fingers creates a "bell" that produces a louder, more ringing sound; closing your fingers produces a more muted sound. Both hands can also be used to create an even bigger bell to magnify the sound. Closing your fingers and holding the call against your chest produces a softer sound. As with a duck call, it's important to maintain air pressure when using the call. Positioning against the lips is important. Place the call to your mouth with the bottom edge of the call gently down on the inside edge of your bottom lip. Next, tilt the call upward until the upper edge touches your upper lip. Maintain just enough pressure against your lips to trap the air and not allow air to escape through your lips or around your call.

Two methods can be used to blow a goose call. You can simply blow into the call like using a large whistle, or you can grunt into the call in the same

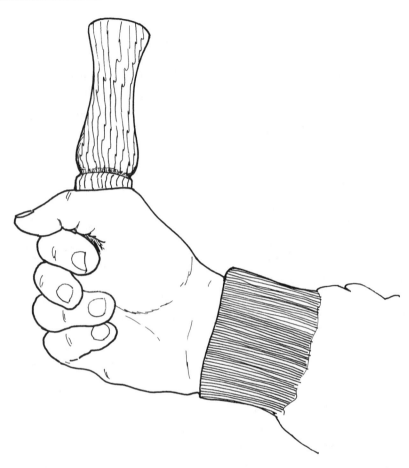

Traditional goose calls are held with your thumb and forefinger, creating a bell with your remaining fingers.

manner as using a duck call. It's mostly a matter of choice. The grunting method provides more volume, as well as allowing for better breath control on long strings of calls. If you call ducks with the grunt method, it's basically the same with goose calling.

Grunting into a goose call is actually forcing your diaphragm upward to force air from your chest into your throat and out the call. Practice holding

Place the bottom edge of the call on your lower lip. Bring the call up against your upper lip to trap all the air.

your breath as you roll your diaphragm upward. You'll feel the buildup of pressure inside your upper chest and throat.

When you blow or grunt through a goose call, like duck calling, you must also say a word at the same time. A variety of words are used for the different sounds geese make. The words that are used with traditional calls for calling Canada geese are WHAT, HA-HA-HA-HA, and HUT. These three word sounds produce the greeting call, feeding call or gabble, and the short honk of Canada geese.

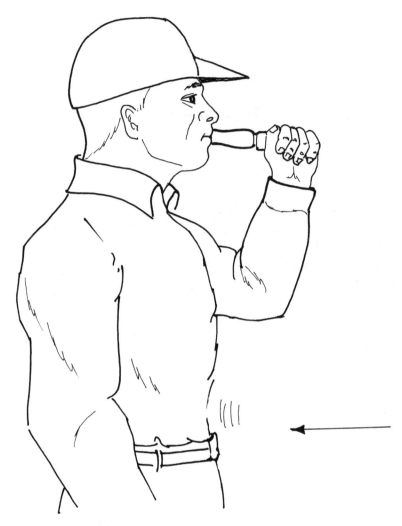

Goose calls can be blown into, or grunted into. At the same time air is introduced through the call, word sounds are used to create the different sounds.

GREETING CALL

Pronouncing the word WHAT while blowing or grunting into the call at the same time produces the honking sound of the greeting call. Starting with fairly low pressure produces the lower note of the two-note sound. Increase air pressure to make the sound break on the higher note. Cut off the air flow at the end of the "honk" with a final T-sound as the tongue stops against the upper teeth.

$$WH \nearrow^{AT} \quad WH \nearrow^{AT} \quad WH \nearrow^{AT} \quad WH \nearrow^{AT}$$

Practice the sound until you can produce the honk. Practice varying the tone and length of the sound. Then learn to make this sound four or five times without taking a breath between calls.

FEED GABBLE

Pronouncing the word HA-HA-HA-HA while blowing or grunting into the call produces the low feed gabbling sound Canada geese make while grazing or feeding. The sound is fairly soft and low. Begin making the sounds very slowly.

HA . . . HA . . . HA . . . HA

Once you learn to make the sounds, gradually speed them up until you can say them very fast and without taking a breath between the string of words. Repeat the sounds numerous times. Closing or opening your hands can add variety to the sounds.

HA-HA-HA-HA-HA
HA-HA-HA-HA-HA
HA-HA-HA-HA-HA
HA-HA-HA-HA-HA

SHORT HONK

Once you have mastered the gabbling sound, proceed to using the word HUT. This a short version of the honk that Canada geese use along with the HA-HA-HA-HA feed gabbling sounds. Begin by saying the words slowly.

HUT . . . HUT . . . HUT . . . HUT.

Then increase the words until you can say them rapidly in a pattern.

HUT-HUT-HUT-HUT
HUT-HUT-HUT-HUT
HUT-HUT-HUT-HUT

HUT-HUT-HUT-HUT
HUT-HUT-HUT-HUT

CALLING PATTERNS

Once you've learned to make the various sounds, they can be used together in calling patterns to call Canada geese into the decoys or into shooting range. It's important to closely observe the flock of approaching geese and match the calling pattern to their response. If the flock is high, quite large, and flying in a V-shape, long sloping line, or check-mark pattern, the geese are called flight geese and often won't respond to decoys or calls.

Small flocks of a half dozen to two dozen geese flying in irregular, compact bunches or milling around are more likely to respond to decoys and calls. Once you spot a distant goose flock with this pattern, give loud "honks" over and over until the flock turns toward your decoy spread.

Once the word sounds have been learned, they are placed in different patterns to match the different calling situations.

WH $\nearrow$ AT   WH $\nearrow$ AT   WH $\nearrow$ AT   WH $\nearrow$ AT   WH $\nearrow$ AT

As the geese approach closer to your spread of decoys, pick up the tempo of your calling.

WH $\nearrow$ AT   WH $\nearrow$ AT   WH $\nearrow$ AT   WH $\nearrow$ AT   WH $\nearrow$ AT   WH $\nearrow$ AT   WH $\nearrow$ AT

As the geese approach to a couple of hundred yards or so, mix in the feed call and gabble with a few well-spaced "honks." Repeat this pattern until the geese have set their wings and are over your decoys or are within shooting range. Closing and opening your hands will provide more variety to the pattern. Some hunters prefer to stop calling when the geese turn into the decoy set, or when they set their wings. Other gunners prefer to keep calling until the geese are just about to land in the spread and the shooting begins. Both methods work; it's mostly a matter of choice, and also the wariness of the geese. You just have to see what works best.

HA-HA-HA-HA-WH $\nearrow$ AT   HA-HA-HA-HA-WH $\nearrow$ AT

HA-HA-HA-HA-HA-HA

HA-HA-HA-HA-HA-HA-WH $\nearrow$ AT

BLEAT CALLING

Bleat calling is an especially effective method when calling geese in the vast midwestern grain fields. Bleat calling consists of a continuous string of "honks" used from the time you see the geese until they set their wings and are heading down into the decoys. This takes a lot of air and effort, and is best done with more than one caller.

WH ↗ AT   WH ↗ AT   WH ↗ AT   WH ↗ AT

As the geese come in closer to the set again, pick up the speed of the sounds.

WH ↗ AT WH ↗ AT WH ↗ AT WH ↗ AT WH ↗ AT WH ↗ AT WH ↗ AT WH ↗ AT WH ↗ AT

In many instances the calls are continued the same right up until shooting time. An alternate tactic is to shift to a very fast feed call mixed with single "honks" after the geese have set their wings but are not quite within shooting range. Given very fast, the pattern produces excited, fast "bleat"-type honks that will bring the birds down fast.

HUT-HUT-HUT-HUT   WH ↗ AT

HUT-HUT-HUT-HUT-HUT-HUT-HUT-HUT

FLUTE GOOSE CALLING

Properly holding a flute call is even more important than a traditional goose call, as the hands play a major part in producing the sounds. Following is the information on using Lohman flute calls. Although different calls may vary somewhat, the basics are the same. The hand that holds the call is called the "On Hand." Place the bell end of the call between the thumb and forefinger of the On Hand. There is a tuft of skin between the thumb and forefinger in this area that is used to partially block the exit hole on the end of the call. Leave the remaining three fingers of the On Hand for producing a connecting circle past the end of the call, creating a bell.

The other hand is called the "Off Hand." It is used for control to provide the extremely realistic goose sounds that flute calls are capable of. Place the top of the thumb of your Off Hand on the back knuckle of your On

Specific patterns are used to attract distant Canada geese, or to work close-in birds.

Both hands are required to use the flute and short-reed types of goose calls. The Off Hand is used to create back pressure to change the tones.

Hand. Allow the remaining four fingers of the Off Hand to wrap around behind the fingers of your already placed On Hand. This creates a cup past the end of the flute call, similar to the manner you cup your hands to drink from a stream.

Advanced callers grunt into the call, but the basic sounds can also be made quite easily by simply puffing out your cheeks and blowing into the call. Again, specific words are used to create the different sounds.

BASIC SOUND

The first sound to learn to say is WHO, and it actually sounds pretty much like a New Year's Eve horn. This is the basic sound that the other sounds are built on. Learn to make the sound steady with no squeaks or breaks in the tone.

WHO   WHO   WHO

If the tone is high pitched, squeaky, or muffled sounding, your hands are too tight and you are choking the call too much. Open your hands slightly. If the sound is garbled or has a fuzzy quality, the hand opening may be too large; in this case you need to choke down on the call or close your hands more. Once you've learned to make the sound clearly and steadily, try it in a series.

WHO WHO WHO WHO WHO

After learning the basics of creating a sound with the call, it's time to move to creating the various calls of the Canada goose.

LONG HONK BLEAT

The long honk bleat is used to attract or get the attention of distant geese. The word used is TOOOOOO-IT, a long, drawn-out sound. Start with the word WHO, then turn it into TOOOOOO-IT. Start the sound fairly low and sharply increase air pressure on the end of the sound to create the higher ending note.

WHO TOOOOOOO-IT TOOOOOO-IT TOOOOOO-IT

Allow a few seconds between honks. This call should be given as loud as possible to get the attention of the geese. As the geese approach closer, speed up the long honks to create an excited sound.

THE CLUCK

The sound used for working close-in geese is the cluck. The word to use in creating the sound is TUT. Some callers prefer to use the word CLUCK, or K-LUK. The latter is a fast two-tone sound. Clucks can be repeated fast or slow depending on the location and reaction of the geese. Normally as geese approach your decoys, the calls should be excited, fast clucks. Once the birds are locked on their final approach, slow down the clucks somewhat. Do not stop clucking, however, as this is a warning to the geese, which usually results in the geese flaring or sliding just out of gun range.

CLUCK-CLUCK-CLUCK-CLUCK-CLUCK-CLUCK-CLUCK—

CLUCK—CLUCK—CLUCK——CLUCK——CLUCK

The K-LUK or double cluck is even more effective, but it requires the correct type of call designed for producing the sound and takes quite a bit of practice. The double cluck is made by producing the cluck sounds very fast and at the same time changing the pitch from high to low, low to high. Smack

"Flute calls don't require grunting; simply blow into them," said Brad Harris of Lohman. "But word sounds must be used at the same time you're blowing into the call."

the call with the air pressure when clucking. The tongue should finish each cluck up and forward in the mouth—as if spitting into the call.

THE COME-BACK CLUCK

If the geese turn away and appear to be leaving, the clucks should be speeded up as fast as possible, creating very excited sounds. The clucks should be extremely close together, extremely fast, high in pitch, and extremely loud.

THE COME-BACK WHINE

The final come-back call, used as a last resort, is the sound given mostly by an old gander to call back the family. The word is TOO-AWWWWWE. The call is a long, pleading, drawn-out sound, like a whine or bawl. Start with a somewhat low volume and increase or exaggerate the sound as the geese continue to leave.

TOO-AWWWWWWWWWWWWWWWWWE

TOO-AWWWWWWWWWWWWWWWWWE

If the flock turns back on the come-back whine, go back into the excited cluck sounds of the come-back cluck.

THE FEED CALL

When geese are feeding, or contentedly resting, they often give a throaty gabbling sound. This sound can be used to let approaching geese know all is well and can also be mixed in with the other calls to produce a very realistic pattern. If one or more callers are working the geese, it's a good idea for one of the callers to continue adding in the feed call.

The word used to make the feed call is HA-HA. Learn to do the call in a fairly rapid but contented-sounding pattern.

HA-HA-HA-HA-HA-HA-HA-HA-HA-HA-HA

PUTTING IT ALL TOGETHER

It's important to continue to watch the geese and change your calling according to their reaction. Geese make a wide variety of sounds, and they are also noisy. If more than one hunter, they should all be calling. Unlike when calling ducks, the sounds made by the hunters can be more imprecise, although sloppy calling isn't as productive as good calling.

Geese can, however, be overcalled. Read the geese; watch their heads. So long as geese continue to approach, keep up the same pattern, but if they start to turn away, change the calling to suit.

CALLING SPECKLEBELLY GEESE

Whitefronted or specklebelly geese are also often called "laughing" or "cackling" geese because their high-pitched calls sound like a person cackling or laughing. Specklebellies also tend to call continuously, whether in flight or especially when landing in a flock of other feeding geese. Their calls are very high and very fast.

Special specklebelly calls are used to make the sounds, and the word used is WAH. Pronounce the word very fast into your call with lots of air pressure to create the high-pitched sound. Learn the word sound, then practice making a long string of calls without taking a breath.

WAH-WAH-WAH-WAH-WAH-WAH-WAH-WAH-WAH-WAH-WAH-WAH-WAH

THE FEED GABBLE

The feeding sound of specklebellies is similar to that of the Canada goose, except faster and a bit higher pitched. The same word HA is used in a long continuous sound without taking a breath.

Whitefronted or specklebelly geese are called in much the same manner as for Canada geese, but with slightly different sounds and patterns.

HA-HA-HA-HA-HA-HA-HA-HA-HA-HA-HA-HA-HA

THE SHORT GRUNT

A short grunt or greeting call is used in conjunction with the feed gabble. The word KU-LUCK is used to produce the sound.

Then learn to put the two together in a pattern.

HA-HA-HA-HA-HA-KU-LUCK-HA-HA-HA-HA-HA-KU-LUCK-HA-HA-KU-LUCK

CALLING PATTERN

Once you learn the basic calls, then it's time to learn a basic calling pattern. When you see a flock of specklebellies, use the laughing honk series three or four times to get their attention.

WAH-WAH-WAH-WAH-WAH-WAH-WAH WAH-WAH-WAH-WAH-WAH-WAH-

WAH-WAH-WAH-WAH-WAH-WAH-WAH WAH-WAH-WAH-WAH-WAH-WAH

When the geese begin to set their wings for their final approach into the decoys, mix in feed calls and short grunts with the honks.

WAH-WAH-WAH-WAH-WAH-WAH

HA-HA-HA-HA-HA-HA-KU-LUCK-HA-HA-HA-HA-HA-HA-HA-HA-KU-LUCK

WAH-WAH-WAH-WAH-WAH-WAH-WAH

HA-HA-HA-HA-HA-KU-LUCK

HA-HA-HA-HA-HA-HA KU-LUCK-KU-LUCK

CALLING SNOWS AND BLUES

Anyone who's watched snows and blues knows they're extremely noisy, especially in the huge flocks they normally congregate in. They also have very high-pitched calls that in flight sometimes sound like the barking of small dogs. The words used for creating their sounds are WHAT, HA-HA-HA-HA-HA, and TUT.

THE HONK

The honk is made by blowing or grunting into the call and at the same time saying the word WHAT. The sound is made in the same basic manner as the honk of Canada geese, cutting off the flow of air at the end of the "honk" with a final T-sound as the tongue stops against the upper teeth. The sound again starts low and ends high, much like that of the Canada goose, but it is faster and higher pitched. Learn to make the sound five or six times without taking a breath between calls.

WH ⌐ AT   WH ⌐ AT   WH ⌐ AT   WH ⌐ AT   WH ⌐ AT

FEED CALL

Like the Canada goose sounds, the feed call is made by repeatedly saying the word HA-HA-HA-HA-HA, creating a gabbling sound. This should be made very fast without taking a breath.

HA-HA-HA-HA-HA-HA-HA-HA-HA-HA-HA-HA

Snows and blue also have similar, but somewhat different sounds and patterns. The sounds, for the most part, are much higher pitched.

FEED HONK

Snows and blues also give a short, very high-pitched honk in with their feeding gabbling. The word used is TUT, and these words are also put into a pattern.

TUT-TUT-TUT TUT TUT-TUT-TUT

All these sounds are then put into a calling pattern that begins with the long honks and changes as the birds approach the decoys.

WH ⌐AT   WH ⌐AT   WH ⌐AT   WH ⌐AT   WH ⌐AT   WH ⌐AT

WH ⌐AT   WH ⌐AT   WH ⌐AT   TUT-TUT-TUT

WH ⌐AT   HA-HA-HA-HA-HA   WH ⌐AT   HA-HA-HA

PRO TIPS

"The most important advice I can give," said Harold Knight, "is to watch and read the goose's wings. Watch their formation and they'll dictate what you need to call to them. Sometimes you need to call extremely fast and loud, and sometimes when the geese get close to the fields and get to circling, you need to tone down your calling. When they start turning and coming in, slow it down, but if they turn and go away, call faster. You need to read the geese, read the wingbeats, watch the formation; that will tell you what you need to do. When those geese are way, way out there, you can't blow too loud. You need to really touch them, and this is where flagging to create movement is very important. I also never call when geese are directly overhead."

"When I do seminars I start off with what you do when you see a flock of geese at a distance," said Kelly Powers. "The call you use when you first see a flock of geese is louder, higher pitched, something to get their attention. It may not even be calling, it may be running through the decoys with a flag or anything. You just want to get their attention. My biggest pet peeve is people who panic when they first see a flock of geese. They throw everything at them

"It's important to watch the geese and how they respond to your calls," said Harold Knight. "Sometimes you need to call fast and loud, sometimes slower and lower." (Photo courtesy Knight & Hale)

"Most people throw all their calls at the geese as soon as they see them," said Kelly Powers. "Then they don't have any 'trump cards' when the geese get in close." (Photo courtesy Avery Outdoors)

at the get-go. Every call they know, they do right at the front. They do get the attention of the geese, and the geese fly toward them. But if those geese don't automatically come in on the first swing, or are a little wary, the hunters have already given all their calls; they don't have a trump card to throw out. It's best to start off with a minimum of calls—just give them what's needed to keep them interested in working the spread. They may work three or four times, then you throw that trump card at them, maybe some come-back calls."

"Most people call way too much," said Fred Zink, winner of over 25 goose calling championships, including the Remington International, Nationals, Grand Nationals, World American, and Grand American. Fred manufactures Paralyzer Waterfowl Calls, is an employee of Avery Outdoors, and does video work for the Mossy Oak Whistling Wing Series. "And they also learn to blow a goose call from maybe a tape or video and then they try to make a lot of different noises. All that is all very well in the beginning when you're trying to learn—a tape or video is excellent—but once you master that technique, then you need to take it to the next level. You need to go listen to live geese, and you need to listen to live geese calling geese. Most people start to call at geese as soon as they see them coming toward them. As soon as the geese appear over the tree line, say 300 or 400 yards away and flying right to them, they start calling as much and as loud as they can. Live geese don't call to other geese in the air until they get around 100 to 150 yards away. If you blow to geese a long way away and they hear that, smart geese will pick up on that and know of possible danger. They know that's not what live geese do, only hunters who have shot their buddies. Most people quit calling at 150 yards. They start at 300 or 400 yards and call a lot, and as the geese get to them at 150 yards, they slow down or actually stop calling. That's actually when live geese start to call to other geese. They get more aggressive, faster, and sharper as the geese get close to then.

"A good caller on average will try to sound like between one and three geese. Most people try to sound like a flock, and they have a human rhythm versus a goose rhythm. Go out and listen to some geese and you'll realize that calling geese like people call geese is a downfall."

"The number one thing with short-reed calls, such as our Mother model, is to get the 'growl' of the goose," said Will Primos. "I call it putting your voice into the call, or humming into the call, and it's necessary in order to get the reed to vibrate at the right frequency to give you the growl of a goose. The growl is especially important in the 'lay-down' call as you try to get them excited when they come in real close. Geese on the ground do that to geese as they come in. A lot of people blow too hard. Good instructions are very important, but you really need to hear the sound.

"Hand manipulation is as important as how much air you put into a call. You can definitely put too much air into the call. When the air comes out of the call you don't want it coming out too fast. If you slow it down, it totally changes the sound the reed will give you. Using your hands to control and manipulate how fast the air is coming out of the call, which is what we call controlling the back pressure, is the other key in learning to use a short-reed call."

Will Primos also gave some good inside information on hunting specklebellies. "Most speck calls that are really loud enough and good enough to carry a long distance in field hunting for specks, you have to blow so hard you get a headache. So we shaved the tip of the reed down on ours. You have the backbone of the reed, which is .00014, and the tip is tapered down to .0006. This provides the volume you need without a whole lot of air.

"Most people call way too much," said Fred Zink. (Photo courtesy Avery Outdoors)

"Most people who hunt specks yodel, a high-to-low yodeling sound. But when specks are way off, I use what I call the piercing hail call. This sounds like TEEEEEE-AH. It is very loud, very piercing, and ranges from high to low. This gets their attention; then when they get close enough, I go to a feed call. I use the word TOO-TOO-TOO-TOO-TOO-TOO. It's more like a peeping sound, very excited, fast, and in a broken rhythm.

"Specklebellies may be the most callable critters I know. They're kind of like turkeys in that they like to be together. They're not like snow geese. Specks are especially callable when you have singles and pairs because they really, really want to get together. You just have to be ready for them. Lots of times you're out in the field duck hunting, speck season is open and you have a speck call with you. It's really neat, they'll readily come to you."

COMPETITION CALLING

"In goose calling competitions you're looking for perfection in a calling pattern," said call contest winner and expert waterfowler Brad Harris of Outland Sports. "You're looking for a series of long-range honking, getting the geese's attention, bringing them your way, getting them excited, getting them over your spread, and once they're over your spread, trying to coax them in. You're going from long-range loud honking, then as they get closer you get into more of the greeting sounds, individual honks, the double clucks, trying to get them excited, wanting to land in your spread. Coaxing them on down with single honks, feed calling. The good contest callers can visualize in their heads the action of the flock of geese they're supposed to be calling."

"It's important to have a good overall flow with your routine," said contest winner Kelly Powers. "A good competition goose calling routine is like a song—it has a flow to it. You also have to be confident of your routine and confident on stage. Once you learn how, it just comes out automatic. But it takes a lot of practice to get to that point—learning to vary with your air pressure, with your breaths of air. It's just like a musical instrument."

"Contest calling starts off with what they call hail calls, which is a long, drawn-out honk," said Fred Zink. "The difference between a contest and the sound of a live goose is there is no such thing in nature. That is just a human perception of what the geese are doing. In reality these geese aren't calling to get the geese to come to them, especially in a feeding situation; they are actually telling them to stay away from my spot, my little piece of real estate."

5

DECOYS

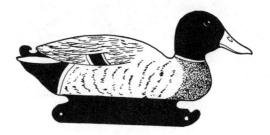

A decoy is a decoy is a decoy—right? That's not particularly true when it comes to a wary old honker, a travel-weary mallard, or when you're packing a ton of decoys across a half mile of plowed, gumbo soil or through a flooded Arkansas bayou. Decoys are available in a wide range of types, and it's important to choose the proper decoy for the most productive and easiest hunting. When I first started hunting waterfowl, there were three kinds of decoys, hand-carved wooden or cork, papier-mâché, and inflatable rubber. Some of those didn't resemble their live counterparts very closely, and some deteriorated before the season was over. With the high-tech, space-age materials available today, decoys are long lasting and are made to match almost any hunting situation you can imagine. Although some decoys are suited to many situations, others are more specialized. Today's decoys have extreme realism in shapes, feather details, and paint. A wide variety of motion decoys have also become available, although some may eventually be banned. Regardless of whether you decoy pintails into a marsh set, mallards into green timber, blue-

Decoys are available of many different materials, sizes, shapes, and for just about any waterfowl species that is hunted.

bills and canvasbacks into big lakes, Canada geese over open water, or snows and blue by the thousands, there are lots of decoys to choose from.

MATERIALS

Decoys have been, and some still are, made of wood and cork. Wood and cork provide the most solid decoys, and those designed and carved correctly provide a "ride" in the water that is the most realistic. They are, however, heavy. They also tend to become chipped and broken over time. Traditional cork decoys are still available from The Decoy Shop. These decoys are honed over 60 years of experience and great for rough-water sets. Herter's also produces handmade cork decoys, featuring a wooden tailpiece and keel. Hard rubber decoys have been produced and they do tend to flex to prevent dents, but very few are available anymore.

The most common decoy material these days is molded plastic. Most of the plastic decoys consist of two sides joined together to create a hollow shell, a one-piece shell, or a silhouette. Molding plastic allows the manufacturer to

Decoys were traditionally made of wood or cork, and some decoys are still made of those traditional materials. (Photo courtesy Fowl Foolers)

create decoys with feathering molded in for extreme realism. Hollow plastic decoys are lighter in weight, fairly economical, and fairly long lasting. They can be broken, cracked, or dented, and they do not stand up to shot. If you accidentally shoot an old wooden decoy, all you get is damaged paint. With plastic decoys you've got a "sinker." Some plastic decoys, such as those from Tanglefree, have plastic blown into them to prevent the problem. The World Famous Herter's Decoys are 100 percent solid-foam-core construction with swivel heads and internal weighted keel. Taking the process one step further, the Herter's Ultimate-Armored Decoy has a patented heat-bonded styrene covering that is chip-, scratch-, and dent-proof. Other solid decoys include Blackwater Rough Water and the Fowl Fooler foam decoys covered with burlap. Herter's also offers burlap-covered decoys.

Plastic foam decoys are also available. These are extremely light in weight, and since they will compress somewhat, a lot of them can be crammed into a decoy bag. We have several public waterfowl wildlife management areas in my state, and some offer "walk-in" hunting only. It's really more like wade-in, but there is also quite a bit of walking. These areas have open-water marsh

The most common material for decoys is hollow plastic. They're lightweight, durable, and can be produced fairly economically.

and lake hunting, and a lot of decoys are needed in order to compete on these popular areas. Some of the really serious hunters haul in 200 to 300 decoys. I found the Feather Flex foam plastic decoys excellent for this situation. I also discovered a huge Remington-brand decoy bag several years ago. It will hold a couple hundred of the foam decoys, and even full, it can be hefted off the ground with one hand. Two of these bags and I'm ready for the competition, regardless of how far I have to pack.

A synthetic rubber decoy is also still available from Carry-Lite. Inflatable rubber or plastic decoys are still available as well. These are extremely lightweight and packable. The Inflata-Coy decoys are made of durable synthetic and collapse for storage. They are self-inflating, and each decoy has a metal ring on the bottom for stabilization and weight. Featherlite decoys are lightweight, self-inflating decoys printed from actual photographs. Both the foam plastic and inflatables, however, are more easily damaged than the solid decoys.

Decoys are also available in plastic foam. These are extremely lightweight, and great for "walk-in" hunting. A large number of these decoys can be crammed into a bag and carried long distances.

DUCK DECOYS

The most common duck decoys are floaters, used for water sets. These may consist of water or weighted keels. Water keels utilize an open design. When the decoy is placed in the water, the keel is submerged and water fills the keel to provide stability to the decoy. Water-filled decoys have a couple of disadvantages. If thrown into the water, often the keel won't roll over and you have to manually right the decoy. They also tend to roll more in rough water and can even tip over. On the other hand, they're much lighter in weight than weighted-keel decoys. You can throw weighted-keel decoys just about any way you want and they'll roll upright. This doesn't mean the decoy string may not loop over the top—a common problem with any type of thrown water decoy. Weighted-keel decoys are much heavier. If weight is a problem—for instance, packing large numbers of decoys some distance— consider water keels. If weight is not a problem, the weighted keels are the best choice.

In addition to the standard, hollow, full-bodied decoys, Flambeau Pontoon Perimeter decoys are actually "half bodied." They have a flat bottom, but are still floaters so they can be used for floating decoys or set on the bank or as field decoys. They feature Lock-Tite swivel heads for multiple poses, and the heads detach for easy stacking and transporting. The Pontoon Perimeter decoys are available in mallard and pintail.

Floating duck decoys are available as either weighted or water keel. Water keels like this one are lighter in weight, but are not as easily set. Weighted-keel decoys ride more naturally. (Photo courtesy Flambeau)

The FUD decoys from Blackwater use a patent-pending construction that allows the full-bodied decoys to be collapsed and carried on a hunter's belt. They are made from lightweight foam laminate; both duck and goose decoys are available. (Photo courtesy Blackwater)

The Flambeau Pontoon Perimeter decoys are half bodied and can be used as floaters or on land.

Field shooting of ducks such as mallards requires field decoys. Floaters can be used, but they don't look as realistic, except when you can push the keel down in the mud. The Flambeau Pontoon Perimeter decoys are great for field shooting. The Herter's Suc Duc decoys have a hollowed-out, concave bottom that creates an air pocket and keeps the decoy stuck to the water's surface, but the flat-bottomed surface allows these decoys to be used as field decoys as well. For extreme realism, and easy packing, the G & H Mallard Shells are hard to beat. These are oversized (20-inch) decoys with a shell design that allows them to be stacked to easily transport dozens to the field. They feature a molded-plastic stake that holds them securely in place and fully adjustable heads. Herter's has duck shells with a unique combination head-stake design that pins the decoy to the ground. The Feather Flex foam decoys can also be used to create extremely large spreads in field situations. The lead dropper weights can be used, or they can be staked. For adding extreme realism to a field set, the Flambeau Enticer Full-Body decoys are hard to beat. Molded to look like a full-bodied duck sitting on a molded base, they offer lifelike detail. They come as a set of four with two drakes and two hens, a feeder and upright head for each, and are simply staked

Shell decoys, such as the G & H Mallards, are easily transported and great for creating large spreads for field hunting.

Feather Flex foam decoys can also be used in the field or as floaters.

The Flambeau Enticer Full-Body ducks add great realism to a field set, placed around the shore on a water set, or placed on the ice.

in place. Just one set added to the spread can offer a great advantage. Carry-Lite also has full-bodied molded flying and landing decoys that can be placed on stakes above the spread for added realism. Herter's Full Body Magnum Field Decoys are great for adding realism to a field spread and will not only attract ducks, but work as confidence decoys for field goose hunting. Mallard shells are also available from Herter's to add to the spread.

DETAILING

I'm really a fanatic about highly detailed decoys, and I've been using G & H decoys for years because of that. Not only is the feather detail great, but the paint pattern is the correct color for the different species and it lasts a long time. The models with swiveling heads can be used to create a much more realistic set with heads turned different directions. I also use Flambeau decoys because of their realism. I like decoys with glass eyes because the eye sparkle adds a great touch of realism. On decoys without that feature, I paint a white highlight in the top of each eye. One of the most interesting decoys is the

Decoys with glass eyes, swiveling heads, and detailed molded feathering, such as these G & H models, offer great realism to a decoy set.

Herter's Millennium. An actual photographic image has been vacuum-formed onto their top-of-the-line 72 Ultimate Decoy. An adhesive base coat fuses the image to the lightweight, hard styrene shell, preventing peeling, chipping, or cracking. Constructed on a solid-foam core, the decoys have swivel heads and are self-righting.

SIZE

Duck floaters are available in standard, magnum, and super magnum. For most situations the standard size is effective. If hunting open water of reservoirs, I go to the magnum simply because they can be seen over longer distances. I haven't used the super-magnum floater duck decoys, although I do know guides who use them in big-water situations. The problem is toting enough decoys to make a decent spread, even in large boats.

In field shooting, I tend to use the larger-sized decoys because they stand out more against the vegetation. We're also usually using some sort of vehicle, such as an ATV, to haul the number of decoys needed for field shooting, so size and weight aren't as important.

SPECIES

Almost all ducks will decoy to mallard decoys, but mallards won't decoy as readily to other species. It is, however, important to match the decoy species to

Duck decoys are available in three sizes—standard, magnum, and super magnum. Shown is a standard-sized mallard drake. (Photo courtesy Flambeau)

Duck decoys are available in many different species. Although most species will decoy to mallard decoys, it's best to match the duck species in the hunting area. (Photo courtesy Flambeau)

the primary waterfowl species in the area. For instance, if you're hunting an area that has mostly pintails, or diver ducks such as bluebills, that's the decoy species you need to be putting out. As an example, in the early teal season I use teal decoys. If the area offers a diversity of species, you can mix the species of decoys, but you should only set them in the natural way the different species react. This will be covered in the chapters on decoy sets.

CONFIDENCE DECOYS

Sometimes other species can act as "confidence" decoys. Because we have lots of resident giant Canada geese in our area, I always use at least a pair of floaters as confidence decoys. Other excellent confidence decoys I've used include great blue heron decoys such as those made by Flambeau. I also sometimes add pintails to a mallard set. Some other confidence decoys I use may seem odd, but one area we hunt has a lot of spoonbills or shovelers. Granted, these are extremely unwary waterfowl, but added to a mallard spread in that area, they help add realism. I've also used coots as confidence decoys on big water. I always add tip-up feeding decoys, at least two to most sets. If the set is on shore, I also add some type of field decoys around the edge of the water. I especially like the Flambeau Enticer Full-Body and Pontoon

Canada goose decoys can act as confidence decoys to duck spreads.

Other confidence decoys include this Flambeau great blue heron and coots.

Perimeter ducks for this. I also use a couple of full-bodied geese set off to one side on the shore.

GOOSE DECOYS

Goose decoys are available basically of the same materials and basic designs as duck decoys, with some additions. Floater geese, as mentioned, can be used as confidence decoys for ducks, but also for water gunning for Canada geese. There simply is no more challenging and exciting form of gunning than bringing Canada geese to the decoys over water.

Again, I look for realism in decoys. Poor-grade goose decoys are not worth the money or the time it takes to set them out. Good decoys are not cheap, however, especially the larger Canada goose models. As I also field hunt for Canada geese, I like decoys that can be used for both purposes. The Flambeau Floater models feature a semiflat bottom with a detachable keel that converts the decoys from floater to field or back to floaters quickly and easily. I also like the Flambeau Floating Canada Goose Shell. These are large,

The Flambeau Floater models feature a semiflat bottom with detachable keel, and have the patented Convert-A-Goose head and neck.

The Flambeau Floating Canada Goose shell is oversized and can be used as a floater or on land.

33-inch-long decoys designed like the Perimeter Pontoon duck decoys and can be used on water or land. All these models also feature the Flambeau patented Convert-A-Goose head and neck assemblies. The neck is designed to be used in either a feeding or sentinel position, by simply swapping ends and inserting the head.

G & H has a unique goose floater that attaches to the bottom of their field shell decoys, quickly converting them to floaters. The Feather Flex goose decoys can also be used as floater or field decoys by adjusting the rigging string or stakes to hold them in position.

A number of hollow plastic floater-type decoys are also available if you don't need the decoys for land sets. G & H has some great-looking full-time floaters. The Cabela's Exclusive Big Foot Floating Decoys offer unrivaled realism. A weighed keel keeps the dekes upright and helps them ride smooth in even the roughest water conditions. A half dozen come with five head styles: one feeder, two resting, one action, one upright, and one alert. Goose dipper decoys are available to add realism to the set. Herter's World Famous Goose Floaters, like their duck decoys, feature a solid-foam body with weighted keels

The G & H shell decoys for use on land can also be used as floaters with a quick detach, attach float.

and swivel heads. Herter's Suc Goose Decoys are also solid foam, but with the Suc-design bottom that allows the decoys to be used in the field as well as for floaters. Lightweight plastic floaters are also available from Herter's.

A lot of goose hunting, for Canadas, but particularly for snows and blues and specklebellies, takes place in feeding fields. The floaters that convert to field use mentioned can be used in this type of hunting situation as well. In addition, many serious hunters like to add full-bodied goose models. These can make a great deal of difference when hunting wary Canada geese. Again, the Cabela's Big Foot models offer great realism. The basic colors are molded in for long life of the decoys, and they are designed to be freestanding without stakes or metal ground inserts, which makes them easier to use on frozen ground. Each set of six includes an active, three resting and two sentry decoys. The Cabela's Goose Swivel Walker keeps the decoys not only headed into the wind, but moving back and forth in a realistic manner. Excellent full-bodied decoys are also available from Herter's, Carry-Lite, Flambeau, and Higdon. Higdon also offers feeder goose decoys with extremely low head styles. The G & H full-bodied goose decoys can be adjusted from feeding to a

Full-bodied goose decoys, such as the G & H shown, can be used as field decoys or placed on the shoreline for water sets.

resting or sentry position by simply changing the head and adjusting the angle of the feet attached to the body. Feet stakes help stabilize the decoys in high winds.

Shell decoys are extremely popular for field uses for many reasons. They're lightweight and, with the heads removed, can be stacked for easy transporting. A hunter can usually tote four to five dozen in a decoy bag. They are also more economical than full-bodied models. Many of the better-quality shell models offer good realism. Excellent shell decoys are available from Carry-Lite, G & H, Herter's, and Flambeau. The Herter's Photographic "Deceivers" Shell Decoys are extremely realistic, with photographic detail and swivel heads.

Field goose spreads require enormous numbers of decoys to be effective, and silhouette decoys are often used to fill in with full-bodied or shell decoys. These are flat decoys on stakes—and you can pack a lot of silhouettes into the field in a hurry. Silhouettes are available from Carry-Lite, Outlaw Decoys, Webfoot Outfitters, and Herter's. The latter three companies offer decoys with photo images.

Shell decoys are lightweight; they can be stacked and big numbers transported to the hunting area fairly easily. The Higdon model shown is extremely realistic.

A thousand or more decoys are needed for field sets for snows and blues, and in this instance rags are often used to add to the set. White diapers were the original rags; plastic garbage bags are also often used. The Texas Rag decoys are made of a waterproof fabric with built-in wing detail and offer a nonshiny finish. At around $30 per 100 for snows, they are an economical method of filling the spread.

SPECIES

Again, it's important to match the species to those hunted. Geese species tend to decoy more readily to their own kind. Specks are particularly hard to decoy to other species; you need a good, extremely realistic set of speck decoys to bring them in. Decoys are available for Canadas, snows, and blues as well as specklebellies from most major manufacturers in floaters, full bodied, shell, and silhouette. Herter's also offers brant decoys. If there are mixed species however, you can create mixed sets.

Where large numbers of goose decoys are needed, silhouette decoys, such as the Outlaw decoys shown, are extremely effective. (Photo courtesy Outlaw)

Feather Flex foam decoys are extremely lightweight and great for creating large goose field spreads.

It's important to match the goose decoy species to the species being hunted.

Goose decoys are also available in three sizes—standard, magnum and super magnum. The larger sizes are best for competing with other hunters in wide-open country. Shown are G & H snow goose sizes.

SIZE

As with duck decoys, goose decoys are available in three sizes—standard, magnum, and super magnum. To give an idea of the differences, the G & H standard shell decoy is 22 inches overall in length, the magnum is 30 inches, and the super magnum is 42 inches. Size does make a difference in many situations, particularly if hunting in wide-open country and competing with numbers of other hunters. The drawback is toting the larger decoys.

MOTION DECOYS

Most knowledgeable waterfowlers know the best way to bring waterfowl in is for someone to leave the blind for a nature call. Many attribute it to bad luck, but some suggest it just might be the motion. In the past, tolling dogs were often used to create motion on the East Coast to attract sea ducks. Regardless, motion can be an extremely important facet in waterfowling success, especially during calm, bluebird days. Some types of motion decoys can also

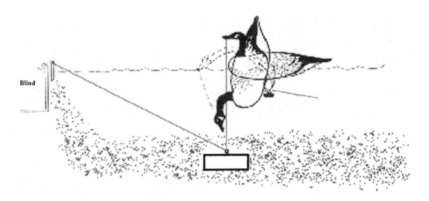

The Finish Floater Canada rig from Higdon is an improved version of the old jerk-cord rig. (Illustration courtesy Higdon)

help prevent decoys from icing over under cold, harsh conditions. Motion decoys consist of manual, or motorized, floaters that are used on water sets, as well as motion-wing models that can be used over water or land sets. The latter are quite controversial and may be banned, because some gunners and waterfowl biologists feel they're too effective.

WATER SETS

A longtime method of creating motion in a water set for either ducks or geese is to use a fairly heavy anchor to hold the decoy in place and run a string from the front of the decoy down to a loop in the anchor, then back to the blind. Jerking on the string causes the decoy to bob forward as if tipping up to feed. Release the string and the decoy bobs back in place, creating ripples on the water's surface. I've been using this tactic for many years, but it does have one drawback. Retrievers tend to get tangled in the jerk line.

The Finisher Floater Canada or snow goose decoy from Higdon is an improved version of the old method. Controlled by an operating cord, this motion decoy can be made to feed at water level, splash water on its back as if bathing, or tip butt-up just like a goose feeding. Twenty-five yards of non-stretch Spectra operating cord are included. A jerk-cord kit is also available from Expedite International. Everything needed is included except for the decoys. Mack's Prairie Wings carries the Yank 'Em In Jerk String Kit featuring a spring-loaded double-action movement.

These days any number of special motion-creating decoys are available that don't require the effort needed to run the string line from the decoy to the blind. One of the most effective I've tested is the Feather Flex Motovator from Outland Sports. Powered by an Attwood water pump, the Motovator vigorously swims around, creating a lot of wakes and ripples. It's powered by six D batteries and features a Feather Flex Magnum Mallard covering.

The Dabbler Duck from Cabela's and Mack's Prairie Wings features a motorized bobbing head and splashing tail that create extremely realistic motion. The Big Head Robotic Decoy has over 20 distinct body, head and neck movements in each 180 degree motion cycle, creating an extremely realistic feeding situation. The Herter's Widow Maker H$_2$O Motion Decoy operates off a remote control and flaps its wings and kicks its feet, creating a great deal of motion. The Real Decoy "Swimmer" duck decoy, from Mack's Prairie Wings, swims just like a real mallard, while their Wonder Duck Decoy features either flapping or rotating wings and can be used in water or land sets. The most impressive water-set motion decoy setup is The Mallard Machine. I first saw it in action at Wildlife Farms in Arkansas. The unit uses a submerged trolling motor prop to make three decoys attached to it dive, bob, swim, shake, thrash water, or sit still. A remote control allows you to operate it from your blind. The Flasher Splasher, exclusive from Mack's Prairie Wings, combines the Mojo Mallard Junior with The Mallard Machine for the most action you can imagine.

Waterfowl are often attracted by the reflection of ripples made on the water, and shaker-type decoys create this type of motion. The Avery Outdoors Wave Maker Decoys provide this motion utilizing a unique stainless-steel pendulum with offset lead head that provides extremely lifelike ripples. With the switch easily accessible on the outside, I've found they are quite easy to use and, most importantly, extremely dependable. They run for up to 30 hours on one alkaline C battery. The Avery Wave Maker Decoys are available in Flambeau and G & H Magnum Mallard, Flambeau Super Magnum, Flambeau Mallard Feeder, and both G & H and Flambeau Canada Goose.

The Quiver Magnet from Expedite International is also an extremely effective and simple motion maker designed to fit into standard-sized floater decoys. Roughly twice as thick as a hockey puck and approximately the same diameter, the device houses an electric motor with an eccentric weighting. Turn it on and it vibrates; place it inside a decoy and presto, the decoy quivers. The

The Avery Wave Maker Decoys shake and wobble, sending out ripples of water through the set.

The Quiver Magnet from Expedite International is a shaking mechanism that can be placed inside hollow decoys.

unit is easy to install—merely cut a flap in the back or top of a decoy, leaving a piece to "hinge" it, pull back the flap, and drop the Quiver Magnet in place. Also available is the Quiver Magnet 2, designed to be attached to an anchor cord and placed directly in the water. It has a molded-in color that becomes nearly invisible in the water, plus a super water-resistant motor. Add three or four of these to your decoy spread and all the decoys surrounding them will "quiver."

The Decoy Heart consists of a counterweight inside a plastic ball. Inserted into a decoy, it creates a random shaking and quivering action, depending on where in the decoy the ball is placed.

LAND SETS

Adding motion is even more important to land sets for ducks or geese. I learned the importance several years ago hunting with David Hale and Harold Knight out of a goose pit located just outside a federal refuge. Those geese were smart. "They can probably name the manufacturer of each decoy,"

Flags, such as from Jackite, are often used in land sets to create motion to attract ducks and geese.

Harold said with a chuckle. One technique, fairly new at the time, however, was productive—flagging. Once a flock was spotted, black cloth flags were waved from the blinds as the callers went into action. Flagging is still a very good technique for sunken blind hunters. It's simple, it doesn't require complicated motion machines, and it works. Black flags are used for Canada geese with white flags for snows and blues. The Flagman T-Flag from Cabela's has two 30-inch wings of ripstop parachute cloth with fiberglass struts mounted on a wooden dowel to produce extremely realistic flagging motion.

These days, however, a number of land-set motion decoys are available that can add more realism to your spread.

Silhouette-style decoys are particularly popular with snow goose hunters who need huge sets, as well as with Canada goose hunters in high-pressure areas. Outlaw Decoys has produced a new model, the Jenny Vane. Using the same patented photographic process Outlaw Decoys is famous for, they are now able to print on a corrugated plastic material. The Jenny Vane design has two important features. First, the weight of the plastic has decreased, making the decoys easier to carry to the field, and making them less costly. A dozen decoys weigh only 4 pounds and can be stacked for easy transport. An additional benefit comes from the staking method. A round metal stake inserted inside the layers of plastic allows the decoy to move with the wind. You can control the amount of movement by how far down you push the stake into the ground.

Chrono Manufacturing also produces some excellent silhouette decoys. Some, including their Robo Goose and Robo Duck, are full-action models. The Robo Goose in Canada or snow goose mimics feeding geese. The double-action body delivers independent head and body movements perfectly imitating a goose walking and feeding. The Robo Mallard uses the same technology, and the drake mallard pivots on a single point, creating a realistic waddling or feeding motion. The Chrono Power Stake is a stake with the movement mechanism, which you can add to any silhouette to add motion.

G & H Decoys produces some of the best, most realistic decoys on the market and their FBWE models—which are available in Canada honker, snow goose, and whitefronted goose—feature manually controlled moving wings, variable head and body positions, and anchorable feet to ensure stability. Operation is simple and effective. Movement of the wing assembly is initiated manually from the pit or blind by a slight tug on the operating cord.

Chrono Manufacturing has some excellent silhouette decoys that can be mounted on their Power Stakes to produce movement.

The G & H Mirage shell goose decoy can be placed on the G & H Motion Stake to create motion with only the slightest breeze. Note the "greeting head."

In addition, G & H has the Mirage full-bodied shell goose decoy, a stackable shell decoy that has the appearance of a full-bodied goose. Oversized with raised feather details for exceptional realism, when assembled in the field, they create an optical illusion or mirage of full-bodied geese. The Mirage also has a Greeter head position that is looking up with an open mouth—greeting the incoming flock. To add realism to the Mirage, G & H has a "Motion Stake" that allows side-to-side feeding motion in light wind.

Higdon Motion Decoys has three models of motion waterfowl decoys for the field. The Full Body Finisher is available in Canada or snow goose pat-

The Expedite International Moto Magnet kit can be used with standard-sized shells or silhouette decoys to simulate feeding birds. A remote model is available. (Photo courtesy Expedite)

terns and utilizes a cord to allow you to create motion of the head and neck, simulating preening or feeding. The Stackable Full Body Finisher features a lifelike motion from the head, neck, and body along with quick and simple field set. The Winged Finishers feature a corrugated plastic wing attached to the side of the Full Body Finisher. The operating cord, attached to the beak, passes through a small eyebolt in the front portion of the wing. As the operating cord is pulled, the Finisher head is drawn downward, pushing the front of the wing down and causing the wing to pivot up, over the back of the decoy. This action perfectly replicates the wing-preening motion of real geese in a relaxed environment.

These moving geese provide many of the benefits of flagging without revealing the hunter's position. Higdon also has a cam system that can be used to operate several of their motion decoys at one time. The operating cords of the motion decoys are attached to the cam arms. The realism provided by several motion decoys increases your odds. The cam system is available in a 12-volt or hand cam model.

Expedite International has a Moto Magnet motion kit that can be added to any full-bodied goose decoy. Their Moto Magnet II is a stake that can be fitted to any standard-sized shell or silhouette decoy. The stake provides a dipping and feeding action with the decoy. The Moto Magnet II Ultra has the same features as the Moto Magnet II, but with remote.

WIND-SOCK AND FLYING DECOYS

Some of the most popular motion decoys are the "wind-sock" style, such as those from North Wind. They inflate even in light breezes and are available in an economy model, allowing you to place a big spread quickly and economically. They are also available in a hovering decoy that is placed on a stake.

One of the most realistic flying decoys is the Jackite. Available in either Canada goose or mallard, these decoys look almost too real in the wind. Attached to a pole with 10 feet of fishing line, they will soar in the slightest breeze. They beat their wings and dip, turn, and glide just like the real thing. Also available from Jackite are fiberglass or bamboo poles for holding the decoys.

Outlaw Decoys has their own version, the Outlaw Kite Decoys, available in Canada goose, snow goose, and mallard. When there is absolutely no wind,

Motion can easily be created on shell or full-bodied duck or goose decoys with Flapperz, lightweight wings that can be attached and flap in even the slightest breeze. (Photo courtesy Flapperz)

these decoys do drop down and hang. Outlaw also has T-Flags that can be mounted on poles to wave and create motion.

The Goose and Duck Magnet models from Expedite International feature a solid-fiberglass head that fits over the pole while the remainder of the body is a wind-sock design. Even without wind they remain in place. With wind they move and flap their wings.

Farm Form Waddler and Super Waddler decoys are constructed of non-glare polyethylene and are stackable for easy transporting. All it takes is a light breeze to rotate these decoys a full 360 degrees.

ROTATING-WING DECOYS

The spinning wings of rotating wing decoys are a great attractant to waterfowl. In fact, there's talk of banning them. They've become so popular a number of manufacturers offer them.

MOTORIZED

Mojo Duck features a large, quiet, direct-drive motor spinning durable, 36-inch-span aluminum wings. Built on realistic Carry-Lite decoy bodies, Mojo Ducks come with 4-foot stake, rechargeable battery, and charger. The Flambeau Sky-Scraper features a direct-drive motor, molded-plastic wings,

A wide range of motorized spinning-wing decoys are available that create the flashing motion of flying ducks or geese. Shown is the Lucky Duck from Expedite International.

RoboDuk also has spinning-wing goose decoys that are extremely effective. (Photo courtesy RoboDuk)

and rechargeable battery, and is available in mallard, bluebill, canvasback, and pintail. The Sky-Scraper also comes with hard plastic carrying case, telescoping stand, battery, and charger. The Expedite International Super Lucky Duck has direct-drive motor and three-piece stake; it operates on a rechargeable battery that is included along with the charger. A remote kit is available. Roto Duck features fold-out wings that eliminate the hassle of attaching wings in the early-morning darkness. Roto Duck also has direct-drive motor, rechargeable battery, charger, and stand. Chrono's Robo Duck and Goose Decoys feature snap-in wing sockets for easy assembly. Their Canada goose model has an adjustable timer and comes with 42-inch pole, battery charger, and carry case.

NONMOTORIZED

Two nonmotorized, rotating-wing decoys are also available. The Tri-Lucky from Expedite is a nonmotorized version that operates by Mother Nature, creating wing movement in winds as little as 7 miles per hour. Higdon's Finisher Flasher operates by hand to spin the wings. Wings spin in one direction while the torsion spring spins them back. Wing keepers ensure that the dark sides of the wings stay up when not in use and that the wings stay in sync with each other.

PRO TIPS

"I used to think motion decoys were a farce," said expert waterfowler Tom Matthews of Avery Outdoors. "But we don't go out without them anymore. They're extremely important if the ducks have been shot at and called to a lot. We put anywhere from six to eight of our Wave Maker Decoys out with three dozen decoys. I tell hunters for every dozen decoys you need at least one Wave Maker, and that's really not quite enough. We use at least two and sometimes three per dozen and we like to put them around the edge of the spread. It seems like that's the first duck they see because it's on the edge. Then we place one or two in the center and this seems to make ripples all through the spread, especially when there is no wind. One miserably slow day several years ago, when we were first getting started with the Wave Maker, we put one out and the only ducks we took were trying to come in and land right on the decoy that was making the motion. It happened time and time again and it convinced us. Since then we've been using them like crazy. I have a couple of places where they work absolutely great. We hunt these little lakes off the river. There are huge willow trees surrounding the lakes and even on a windy day, when you get back in the corners with the wind at your back like you should be, you can look out a 100 yards across the lake and see ripples, but it's dead calm back in the corners. The Wave Makers really work great in those situations.

"I also think motion is extremely important on overshot and overcalled ducks. We've gotten to the point where we don't even call. They just see the motion and it works.

"Our tip-up-style feeder motion decoys really make a difference, as does our teal motion decoy. Not only is this important for those who like to get in on the annual 'first-of-the-season' hunt in many states, but we've also discovered the small teal decoys seem to really put out a lot of motion.

"I feel people overcall and underdecoy, and the motion made by the Wave Makers can really make a difference. Many of us have lost the art of setting decoys. We just toss them out any old way, but there is an art to it. I've seen experts go out and move a decoy 3 or 4 feet and really make a difference. Motion decoys kind of take the 'art' out and make decoy setting easier."

6

DECOY RIGGING AND TRANSPORTING

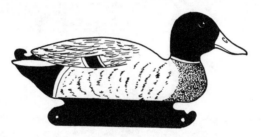

Setting out decoys can be a chore even under the best of conditions. Trying to untangle and set out a jumbled mess of duck or goose decoys and lines in the early-morning darkness with the temperature hovering just above freezing is utter frustration. The chore has made most waterfowlers swear and some decide to quit. With proper rigging, however, setting out and retrieving duck or goose decoys can be much easier. A number of rigging products have also made the chore easier.

RIGGING LINE

The biggest problem is weights coming loose from the decoys and entangling the lines. Or if the lines aren't properly wrapped on the decoys, they can also become loose and tangled. For a number of years tarred or black, brown, or green cordage was used for decoy anchor lines. It is still used by some traditionalists, as well as for deep-water sets and for gang rigging. This

Proper decoy rigging is necessary for ease of use and productive hunting.

Decoy line is available as dark brown or green cordage, or these days in plastic. The easiest-to-use line is Tanglefree, made of solid PVC.

type of cordage is also available braided with several colors and is a good choice for heavy decoys such as goose or magnum duck, and especially on big waters that can have a lot of wind and wave action.

Tanglefree line solves both of these problems quite easily. The Original Tanglefree decoy line is a solid PVC type line, dull green in color with a tensile strength of 1,500 psi. It will not freeze, rot, or flare ducks, and resists tangles when used with Tanglefree decoy anchors. Anchors are ¼ ounce in weight, and no knots are needed when securing Tanglefree decoy line to Tanglefree decoy anchors. The plastic decoy line snap secures the line to the decoy with a snap of the fingers; no tools are required.

DECOY ANCHORS

A wide variety of anchors are available, and it's important to choose the anchor to fit the hunting situation. Most anchors are made of lead, and some are also available with a plastic coating. The plastic coating not only protects the anchors from becoming scratched or nicked—which can damage the decoy finish—but also prevents you from handling lead, which can be dangerous when handled over a period of time.

The most common lead decoy styles are strap, mushroom, and loop. The most economical and popular are the strap styles. These are soft and are bent around the neck or keel of the decoy. They tend to stay on the neck more readily than the keel, but over time will scratch the decoy neck finish. Mushroom weights are similar and are also wrapped around the neck. They feature a thin round shank with a mushroom head for better holding power in high winds. Mushroom weights are also available shaped like miniature boat anchors or with a lead bottom and wire loop at the top. The boat anchor styles are most commonly removable, as they can't be fastened to the decoys neck or keel. The loop/mushroom types can be placed over the decoy head. Another loop type is a flat round oval of lead with protrusions on each end. This provides more holding for heavier decoys and also slips over the head.

Greenhawk Decoy Anchors are of this style, but also feature a unique bottom edge that causes the weight to tip over once it hits bottom—and then it digs in for even more holding power. Ace Decoy Anchors are designed to snap on and off keels rather than being placed around the neck, preventing damage to the decoy finish. DukshU Decoy Anchors are rubber coated, shaped like a

Mushroom

Strap

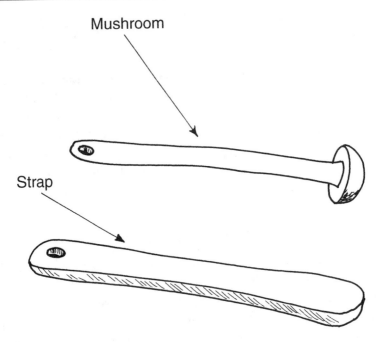

Decoy anchors vary according to where and how they are used. Strap weights are the most common for pothole and sheltered water sets. Mushroom weights tend to hold better and are best for areas with high winds and waves.

horseshoe to fit over the decoy keel, and also have a stainless-steel spring to keep lines taut when wrapped in place. G & H Decoy Anchors are quite unusual in that they are molded of high-impact plastic and are hollow. They must be filled completely with sand or shot to produce the weight; they nest under the decoys on the keel. Intruder Decoy Anchors are also somewhat unusual. Shaped like a cone, they fit over the decoy bill. Your decoys won't drift even in high winds due to the scooping action of the decoys. And they also have a stretch elastic strap that helps absorb the shock of high waves. I found them great, even on some big Flambeau Canada goose floaters.

You can also make your own mushroom-style lead anchors quite easily. You'll need lead, which can be from any number of sources, including old pipe or wheel weights. You'll also need a small iron ladle and a blowtorch. Bend a piece of galvanized, No. 9 wire into a loop that will fit over the decoy head and bend a hook on each end. Place lead chunks in the iron ladle and use the torch

A hollow plastic G & H anchor can be filled with lead or shot and snaps directly onto the decoy keel.

Intruder Decoy Anchors are shaped like a cone and won't drift even in high waves. The cone fits over the decoy bill when not in use.

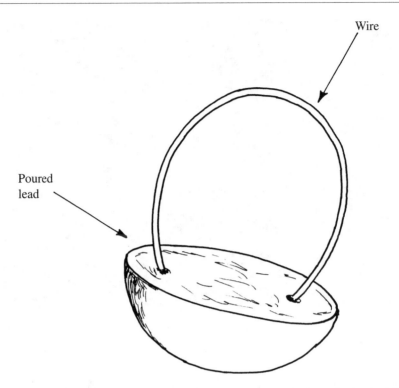

Wire

Poured lead

You can also make your own lead mushroom-style anchors. Bend a loop of galvanized No. 9 wire that will fit over the decoy head. Place the wire in a steel ladle and melt lead with a torch to form the anchor.

to heat the lead to melt it. Once the lead liquefies, place the loop into the melted lead and allow the lead to cool. You'll have to experiment to determine the amount of lead needed to make a weight of the size needed to hold your particular decoys. *Note:* Melting lead is dangerous. Protect your body with long clothing, heavy leather gloves, and eye protection. The fumes from melting lead are also dangerous. Do this job outside and wear a respirator mask.

SINGLE RIGGING

With weights or anchors and cordage selected, the next step is to fasten the weights to the decoys. The traditional method with cordage is to simply use a doubled overhand knot to tie the cord to the weight, then attach the cord to the decoy keel in the same manner. Decoys have holes in both ends of the keel so all the decoys don't face the same direction and you can add variety to your spread. I like to tie two out of a dozen decoys in the back hole.

Ideally the string should be long enough to allow the decoy to swing a little in the wind and waves, but not overly long or the decoys will swing around each other, entangling the strings. Too short a string length can, however, pull up the anchors in high wind and waves. The lines should actually be about two and a half times the water depth. For 2 feet of water, a line length of 7 feet is about right. Bad weather and rising tides can also increase water depth, so you need to be ready for those problems as well. Chasing rigs that have broken away in high winds and rough water is no fun—as I've discovered more than once.

The big problem is that decoy string lengths must vary according to water depth. Even if you hunt the same water all the time, there will usually be some depth variation. The strings should be cut, then tied at the longest length of working depth you expect to encounter. You can shorten the decoy strings by simply unwinding only the amount needed, then tying a loop knot around the keel protrusion on the front of the decoy. When cutting cord lengths, cut an experimental length and tie off to the decoy and weight. Adjust the length until the weight will fit snugly in place over the head or to the keel when all line is wound in place. Once you establish the correct length, cut all cords to the same length, then tie the cords to the decoy keel holes and weights. Tanglefree Decoy Line Clips make this chore easy, and they can be used for single decoys or multiple use with gang rigs. Merely snap the line clip in place.

A number of decoy cord adjusters, used to fasten the line to the decoys, have made the chore of lengthening or shortening decoy cords to suit the situation much easier. The Greenhead Adjusters from Avery Outdoors slide up and down on the cord, eliminating winding and unwinding cord when the depth of the water changes. Simply slide the adjuster up or down the cord to the desired length.

The Decoy Rigging Kit from Cabela's has everything you need to rig decoys the easy way. The kit, which does a dozen decoys, includes 100 feet of Quick-Fix plastic decoy cord, 12 strap weights, 12 decoy cord depth adjusters, and 12 decoy cord crimps. Plastic decoy cord does have a tendency to "untie," and the crimps make fastening the cord to the anchors extremely easy.

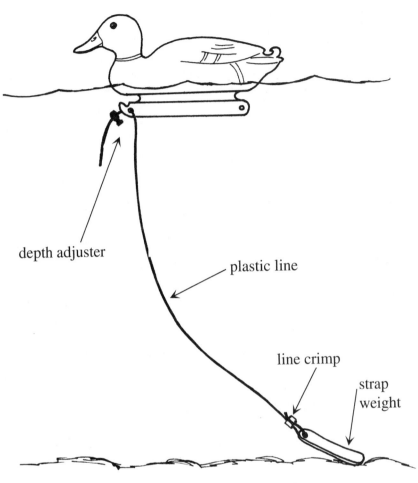

depth adjuster

plastic line

line crimp

strap weight

The Greenhead Decoy line and adjustable clips make rigging quick and easy and you can adjust the depth of the weight by sliding the clip.

First step with the kit is again to determine the longest length of cord needed. Then thread the crimp on the plastic cord, run the cord through the hole in the strap weight and then through the crimp. I also like to tie an overhand knot in the cord end protruding through the crimp. Pull the knot back, then smash the crimp. A pair of locking pliers makes the chore quick and easy. Thread the cord through the hole in the decoy keel, then in the adjuster.

The Greenhead Gear Decoy Rigging Kit from Avery comes with everything needed to rig a dozen decoys, including 100 feet of Quick-Fix PVC decoy cord, strap weights, aluminum cord crimps, and decoy cord depth adjusters. It's the easiest rigging I've used.

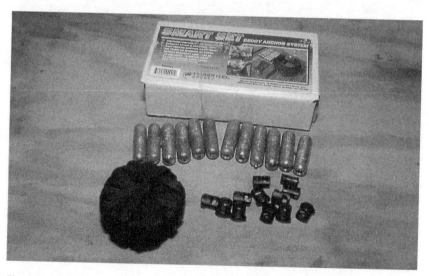

The Smart Set Decoy Anchor System is designed for the Feather Flex decoys and can be rigged to create a floating or field set. It comes with tangle-resistant line, anchors, and push-button cord locks.

GANG RIGGING

Most puddle duck sets consist of decoys rigged individually. Diver sets can, however, utilize multiple or gang-rigged sets. Gang sets consist of one line to which several decoys are attached. Several advantages are offered for deep-water diver sets with this technique. The most important is that only one or two anchors are used, instead of multiple anchors, thus preventing tangling of the decoys on long lines. This also means less time setting and pulling decoys. I use the gang, sometimes called "mother rigs" or "long lines," in combination with individual decoys when setting combination puddler, diver sets in open water. Gang rigs are also a good choice in current as they don't tangle as easily.

Manufactured gang rigs are available. The Cabela's Decoy Gang Rig consists of 28 feet of ⅛-inch black polyethylene line with built-in polyurethane stops spaced 4 feet apart. The decoys are attached to heavy-duty brass swivels. The Cabela's Gang Rig Kit utilizes 100 feet of 300-pound-test nylon cord and 12 stainless-steel spring-loaded decoy anchor snaps. A malleable iron 1½-

Diver and sea duck decoys are often gang rigged. This consists of a single line with a weight on one end, or weights on both ends, and the individual decoys fastened to the main line.

PVC line can be used for the main line, with loops formed for the individual decoys. Special clips are available, or use clips from an old fish stringer.

pound anchor with a hot-dipped galvanized finish folds and locks in the open and closed positions. Spring tension keeps the snaps from slipping on the cord so your decoys stay in the spread as you arranged them.

You can also make your own gang rigs quite easily. Sturdy, dark nylon or plastic cordage may be used. The latter, however, has a tendency to become overstretched in extremely rough water. Because my gang rigs are positioned out ahead of the regular set, I normally use at last 100 feet per dozen decoys.

Manufactured gang-rig kits are also available, such as the kit shown from Cabela's. (Illustration courtesy Cabela's)

The rig can consist of an anchor on one end, or an anchor on each end. The former is set by anchoring into the wind and allowing the line to sway back and forth with the wind and waves. Anchoring both ends prevents entanglement but does not provide motion that is quite as natural. Tie an overhand loop knot in the main line at the locations you want to place the decoys. Shower curtain hooks can be used to fasten the decoys in place to the line. First attach one end to the decoy tie hole. Snap-style fish stringers can also be dismantled and used for the chore, as can large brass trotline swivel hooks. The snaps are installed on the decoys and left in place. When you wish to set out the rig, simply place the snaps over the loops in the line. If you wish to provide more concealment to the main or mother line, tie a foot of dropper line to the decoy tie hole, then add the snap hook. This drops the main line below the water's surface.

RIGGING GROUND DECOYS

Ground decoys consist of shell- and silhouette-type decoys. Many shell-type ground decoys are simply set on the ground, but even the heavier can get blown about in high winds. Some shell decoys can be rigged with a short section of line and a weight. Other shell decoys utilize a stake. Silhouette decoys also require staking.

Setting out stake decoys, especially those with fat plastic stakes, requires a steel hole punch to create the holes in the ground. I've discovered when setting out several hundred stake-type goose decoys that the best tactic is to have one hunter drive the holes, while another or (even better) two hunters follow and set the decoys in the holes. Outlaw has a steel hole punch with a handle and foot peg that allows your full body weight to make the ground holes. If the ground is extra hard, rock the handle back and forth while standing on the foot peg and work the punch into the ground. In soils that cave in and fill the hole as you remove the punch, place the stake against the punch as you are removing it. Then, as the punch clears the hole, immediately push the stake into the hole before cave-in occurs.

The Feather Flex goose decoys from Outland Sports are basically foam plastic and come with thin wire stakes that are pushed though the top of the decoy and into the ground. Not only are the decoys extremely lightweight, but

Most shell or silhouette decoys utilize some sort of stake.

they are really quick to set out in this manner. When hunting snows and blues, you can set out several hundred decoys in minutes. I keep the stakes separate from the decoys in a hard plastic tackle box. Simply pull the decoys out of the bag and jam the stake in place.

Silhouette decoys, such as those from Outlaw, can be used on water as well as land with a little ingenuity. If the water is shallow, ¾-inch plastic PVC pipe can be cut into the lengths needed and simply pushed into the mud, then the decoy stakes set in the pipe. Plastic pipe makes hunting in 2 to 4 feet of water a simple matter. If hunting in deep water, homemade wooden V-boards can be used to hold the decoys. These also work quite well on frozen ground. One of the problems in using stake decoys is frozen ground or ice. According to the folks at Outlaw Decoys, you can use plastic pipe in fields to create permanent holes in frozen ground for your decoys. It will cost about five cents per decoy to install permanent, plastic pipe holes in a field. Some hunters use cordless, battery-powered drills to make stake holes in ice or frozen ground.

MOTION DECOYS

A variety of motion decoys are available, and they require somewhat different rigging tactics. Most spinning-wing decoys come with a metal stake that is pushed in the ground or mud, and the decoy placed on the stake. Some stakes have a step welded on to help push the stake into the ground. You can also weld steps onto those that do not have them. Most stakes are fairly short; if you're hunting in deeper water, one solution is to drive a long pipe in place, then position the decoy stake in the pipe.

Floating motion decoys are rigged in the same basic method as the regular floaters. In some instances, however, you may wish to use larger anchors to keep the decoy movement from shifting or pulling the anchor loose.

Motion decoys are not new. In fact, they've been around for many years. The traditional method utilizes a decoy on a string controlled from the blind. They can add a lot of action to a lifeless spread, especially on those calm, windless days. Almost any type of floater decoy can be used for the tactic, but water- or hollow-keel decoys aren't quite as effective as those with weighted keels.

The first step in creating the motion decoy is to drill a tiny hole in the end of the decoy's beak. Insert a small screw eye and epoxy it in place to make sure it is secure or attach the string to the keel. The next step is to fasten three or four anchors together with a wire loop. Position a snap swivel over a length of 50-pound-test monofilament and tie a snap swivel to the end. You'll need enough monofilament to reach from the decoy to the blind. The line can be wound and stored on a thin board, but the best tactic is to use an old or inexpensive closed-face spinning rod and reel. Simply cut the rod off in front of the handle. This makes it easy to store the line untangled as well as easy to set out and retrieve. To set up the decoy, fasten the snap swivel on the end of the line to the screw eye on the decoy bill or keel. Fasten the snap swivel that is loose on the line to the wire loop holding the anchors together. Lower the anchors in place and unwind the monofilament back to your blind.

When you see ducks in the area, or even if you can't see them, tug on the monofilament line and the decoy head will bob under the water like a duck tipping up to feed. When you release the monofilament, the decoy will sit back upright with a slight splash. "Swimming" decoys can also be rigged in a similar manner.

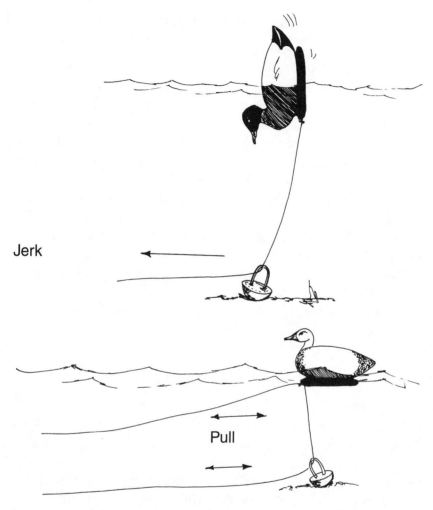

You can create your own simple floating motion decoy with a jerk string. The way the string is fastened can create a dabbling or swimming duck.

Rigging decoys can be a fun way of passing a winter evening after the season is over, getting everything ready for the coming season. Most of us, however, end up doing it late at night the evening before the opener. Regardless, properly rigged decoys can be pleasurable to use and extremely productive.

PRO RIGGING TIPS

"The type of rigging generally depends on where I'm hunting," said Brad Harris of Outland Sports. "In most marsh, pond, or timber situations I just use standard rigging. About the only time I get creative with rigging is when river hunting in current. I rig the front decoy on one end of a 50-foot heavy green cord with a drop and a heavy anchor. Then I step back every 3 or 4 feet and tie my floaters directly to that line. The current holds the one decoy in place, and the floaters drift back behind. You can do this with multiple pieces of cord or one piece of cord, depending on how big the water is.

"I use lead drops on the Feather Flex foam decoys, and they are so versatile. I pull them up tight to the neck and use them in shallow-water and field situations. I also take the Feather Flex foam decoys that come with a wire stake and instead of rigging them with standard drops on weights, I stake them in very shallow water or for ground operations. I run the wire stake through the front or breast of the foam decoy about an inch, back out, and straight back to the ground. In any kind of wind the decoys look like they're walking. The foam decoys staked in that manner in field situations really give a lot more movement."

TRANSPORTING DECOYS

Getting decoys to and from hunting spots takes work, particularly with large numbers of decoys. Regardless of whether you're taking a half dozen dekes back to a flooded timber set or several hundred dekes to an open rice field, you'll probably need decoy bags to organize and hold the decoys. Most longtime waterfowlers have their rigging and decoy bags tightly organized. This prevents problems when setting out decoys in the early-morning darkness.

Decoy bags are available in several different sizes and made of a variety of materials. Different designs are also available for different types of decoys. Don't buy the inexpensive, netting bags, as they won't last the season. I've tested the better bags from Avery, Hunter's Specialties, G & H, and Cabela's, and they all feature extra-tough netting materials for long life. Features vary according to the design. Square-bottomed bags from Avery and Cabela's make loading decoys easier. Cabela's also carries a "pop-up" bag that has an internal wire frame to hold it upright for easy loading. If carrying decoys on your back, a bag with comfortable shoulder straps is necessary. The Elite Decoy Bag from

Quality decoy bags are a must. Make sure they are extra sturdy.

Cabela's has a padded foam back, shoulder straps, and belt. It fits and carries more like a backpack and will carry up to three dozen decoys.

Decoy bags range in size from the Avery 12-pack bag, which is small and carries just a dozen decoys to those backcountry spots, to the huge Cabela's two-man carry bag for toting a large number of shells or large floaters.

In addition to the standard decoy bags, Avery also has a Rag Bag Decoy Bag for toting goose rag decoys. It will hold up to 200 rags and stakes in a secure bundle. Silhouette decoy bags are designed to hold silhouettes with stakes attached, and are available from Final Approach and Avery. The Avery bag is a poncho style to carry decoys in both front and back.

Decoy bags can be used to transport decoys, or to keep them organized for storage. In some cases, however, means other than toting on your back may be used for transporting decoys. Decoy sleds are available that can be used to slide large numbers of decoys over frozen ground, mud, or grass. Some sleds are also floaters, enabling you to float large numbers of decoys to water locations; they can easily be pulled while wading through shallow water. The Cabela's Floating Coffin Blind not only can be used to float decoys through shallow water, but provides a lay-down blind when you get to your hunting

Specialty decoy bags are available such as the Avery Poncho for carrying silhouette decoys.

You will need a variety of sizes and shapes for the different decoys.

spot. Larger models of floating sleds can also be used behind waterfowl boats. Cabela's Sportsman's Sled will hold up to 10 dozen standard-sized decoys.

If transporting decoys over dry land, but in areas where vehicles are not allowed, a lightweight wheeled cart can be used. Several are available, including the Decoy Dolly from Cabela's. The dolly can hold up to five dozen duck decoys without breaking your back, and the two 16-inch wheels easily roll over even rough terrain. The Decoy Dolly floats in 18 inches of water and can also be quickly converted to a two-person bench seat or a one-person layout chair. The Decoy Dolly can be used to haul out deer and other downed game and comes with its own 38- by 58-inch decoy bag.

Another excellent cart is the all-aluminum API game cart. Although designed primarily for carrying out deer and other big game, it features a heavy-duty mesh carrying system and folds up compactly for storage and transportation.

One of the easiest methods of transporting decoys is on an ATV, utility vehicle, or amphibious vehicle. Decoy bags can be tied to the front and rear racks of ATVs. When transporting several hunters plus several hundred decoys, I often tie the decoys to racks on my truck, as well as inside the truck bed,

In areas with nonvehicular regulations, lightweight, two-wheel carts such as the API cart shown are ideal for hauling bags of decoys.

In areas where legal, ATVs or utility vehicles, such as the E-Z-Go shown, can haul loads of decoys and hunters.

Amphibious vehicles such as the MAX IV can haul hunters, gear, and tote trailers full of decoys.

and pull a trailer loaded with the ATV. The ATV has a ball hitch attached to match the trailer. At the hunting location I drive the ATV off, unhitch the trailer from the truck, hitch it to the ATV, and then tote hunters, gear, and decoys. This is an especially effective tactic when transporting large numbers of decoys, layout blinds, and hunters to the goose field.

All-terrain utility vehicles, which feature off-road, four-wheel-drive capabilities, such as the Kawasaki Mule, E-Z-GO WorkHorse, Club Car Pioneer, Polaris Ranger, John Deere Trail Gator, Columbia ParCar Scout, and Arctic Cat SBS 1000 are great for the chore. They feature two-across seating, drive like automobiles, and the back bed can be used to carry large numbers of decoys. Amphibious vehicles such as the ARGO and Recreative Industries MAX are perfect for not only transporting decoys, but also getting just about anywhere you can imagine to hunt.

7

DUCK DECOY SETS

Seeing a quick movement in the sky to your left, you hunker lower and hug the rough bark of the oak. As you shift your weight, water sloshes around you, and the tingling trickle of more icy water sifts down inside your chest waders through the unfound pinhole. A slab of ice drifts up against your side; your toes are completely numb. You hardly notice, however, because the lead hen of a huge flock of mallards is now spiraling down out of the storm-tossed sky into the small patch of water in front of you. You ignore the call hanging at your chest; you don't need it now. You swirl your foot around to create a little water motion, then stand motionless, a part of the gray, drab, cold landscape.

With rustling wings that block out all other sounds, they come in. Ten, 15, then 50 more, maybe 100. You can't even guess at the number of huge red-legged greenheads dropping out of the sky into this small pocket of open water. With pounding heart, you watch the spectacle before you. Your hands are shaking more from the excitement than the cold. Birds are settling down, talking to each other with the noisy, neighborly chatter only a flock of travel-weary mallards can make, and rocking the dozen dekes floating in the icy water. The bright mallards shift, reshift, and flutter up, in constant motion, and still you're hunkered only 25 yards away, frozen to the icy tree trunk. You already have a couple of mallards floating in the water on a thong tied to your waders, and only need a couple more birds for your limit. But you become mesmerized as the big flock continues to funnel in.

You've got to move or freeze in place and become a permanent part of this tiny hole of water in the middle of a frozen marsh. You unsteadily bring the gun to your shoulder and shout at the top of your lungs. At first the startled birds look for danger, then with a roar of wings and a thrashing of water, they're off and climbing for altitude. You pick a drake coming directly over your head and pull the trigger. He keeps going. Your cold, numbed hands almost refuse to work, but you keep tracking and a second shot tumbles him. Then you spot another drake, climbing to the left, and a lucky shot drops him as well.

Eagerly you wade toward the birds, thankful for the action to warm your body. Feathers are floating down all around from the mass of ducks winging over-

Decoying ducks is a major facet of waterfowling. It is not a mysterious art, but does require some basic knowledge, and usually lots of hard work for success.

head, and waves of water are still rippling out past you. You gather up the decoys, stuff them hurriedly into a bag, and start back through the marsh to your vehicle. You're cold and tired, but happy, as only a successful waterfowler can be. You also have a memory that will last a lifetime of all those birds settling into your decoys.

Decoying ducks, whether mallards to a secluded slough, pintails over a marsh, bluebills off a windswept rocky lake point, or wood ducks into a flooded timber pothole, is the ultimate in waterfowling. Granted, calling is a very important part of waterfowling, but I think for the most part calling is overrated. A waterfowler can attract and kill ducks without a call. I've done it many, many times, including the hunt just described. I've also more than once fallen asleep in a blind only to awaken and find my decoys loaded up with birds. Ducks can also become extremely call-shy. You can't, however, successfully bring in waterfowl without decoys.

Decoying waterfowl isn't so much a mysterious "art" as it is hard work. A basic understanding of how the various species of waterfowl react to the various decoy spreads and how they approach the decoys is, however, necessary.

Following are specific decoy spreads for a variety of water conditions as well as for the different species. These are general suggestions; you don't have to adhere exactly to the number of decoys shown, or the exact placement. In fact, as the conditions change—wind direction and so forth—you will have to adjust the set to suit.

But first, a bit of waterfowl knowledge is important. Like planes, ducks must land into the wind. The airflow created by the wind over their wings allows them to glide or maneuver. Decoys must be set so the birds have a place to land into the wind. Second—and this is the first rule of successful waterfowling—you have to be where the ducks want to be. A thousand decoys set up in the wrong place won't bring in a flock of ducks. A half dozen decoys, set where the ducks want to be, can be just the enticement needed.

Even if you're in the right place, simply tossing out decoys in a random pattern is usually not the most productive method. Most gunners use a pattern or patterns that suit their gunning situations or the timing of the season. Traditional patterns are based on either a C-, J-, or V-shape. In all instances the opening faces with the wind. This allows the birds to come in and land in the pocket created by the decoys without having to fly over the decoys, which most species don't like to do. These patterns are not set in stone, but will vary somewhat according to the situation and even from locale to locale.

The first rule is, ducks must land into the wind. The decoys must be positioned to allow a landing pocket against the wind.

It's also important to set your decoys to provide the best shooting. This is often more a matter of blind placement than of decoy placement, but with permanent blinds, it's often impossible to change blind positions. In this case, the decoys must be more strategically placed. If possible, have the decoys and blind positioned so the birds swing across in front of your blind, rather than coming straight in or from the back over the blind. This isn't always possible, but it does provide the best shooting positions and also prevents birds from coming straight in, as they tend to be more wary of the blind. If you're a right-handed shooter, the best scenario would have the birds coming from your right side, as most right-handed gunners swing better to the left.

The next step is to make sure you position marker decoys at the outside limits of your shotgun, loads, and shooting ability. Normally this will be 35 yards. Granted, shots are taken at longer distances, and sometimes made, but often the results are cripples, especially with steel shot. In most gunning situations it's a good idea to also place the outside edge of your decoys within 35 yards. This helps to prevent ducks from landing outside the decoys—a common problem, especially in mid- to late season on decoy-shy ducks.

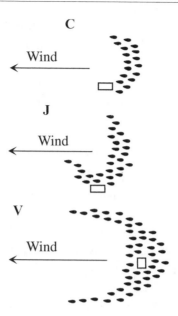

Puddle and diver duck decoys are normally deployed in one of three basic patterns; the C-, J-, or V-shape, with the opening facing with the wind.

Set your decoys for the best possible shooting. The best scenario is to have the birds swing across in front of the blind before settling into the decoys.

The way the decoys are dispersed—close or scattered—can also vary a great deal. This depends on the timing of the season and other factors and will be discussed in later chapters.

Following are some basic patterns for different situations. Remember, these must be varied according to the wind direction and other factors.

POTHOLE OR MARSH SET

Puddlers, such as mallards, pintails, gadwalls, widgeon, and teal, are the most common waterfowl in small potholes. This is one of the most commonly used sets for shallow-water, small pockets of ponds, sloughs, and marshes. The spread is set in small open pockets of water in the vegetation. The size of the pockets can vary from 100 yards or so wide to several acres, but the pockets are typically isolated with lots of vegetation surrounding them. This is classic, but easy waterfowling. Farm ponds are also set in the same basic style. Some of the most successful waterfowling I've experienced has, in fact, been on farm ponds with this type of set.

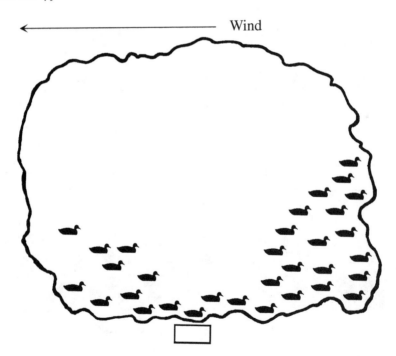

The basic pothole or small marsh set. Can also be used for farm ponds.

The number of decoys needed will vary according to the size of the pothole, the amount of hunting pressure, and the time of the season. For instance, during the early part of the season, only a handful of decoys may be needed. As the season progresses, ducks become more wary, the flocks coming to these secluded areas are larger, and more decoys are sometimes required. At times, however, local ducks become decoy-shy later in the season, and cutting back on the number in a spread is more effective. For the most part, a spread of one to three dozen duck decoys is usually considered effective. Confidence decoys can be great blue herons standing in the grass, or pintails for mallard sets. Placing a group of a half dozen gadwalls just outside the decoy spread also adds realism.

Depending on the size of the opening in the vegetation, decoys are placed around the edges in a U- or V-pattern with an opening in front of the blind. It's best to have the wind blow across in front of the blind rather than directly into or away from it.

BIG MARSH SETS

Depending on the size of the marsh, the same basic sets are used, but with larger numbers of decoys. Magnum models are typically used. This is one scenario on a walk-in public waterfowl area near my home. Large numbers of decoys are needed, and lightweight plastic foam models are often the best choice. In this case 300 to 400 decoys is not an unusual number. Create a large C- or oval shape with a pocket in front of the blind.

RIVER SETS

Rivers are used by all species of waterfowl as travel corridors, as well as for resting and in some cases feeding areas. River sandbars, backwaters, and sloughs can also provide some extremely productive waterfowling. The size of the river dictates the number of decoys. Larger rivers will require more decoys; small creeks and rivers fewer blocks. Anywhere from one to four dozen is normal on medium to small rivers. Rivers tend to be resting rather than feeding areas, and the decoys should be dispersed to appear as contented and resting. A C- or hook pattern with a handful of decoys located on the sandbar or point is the most productive. In current situations long-line rigs positioned with the

Wind

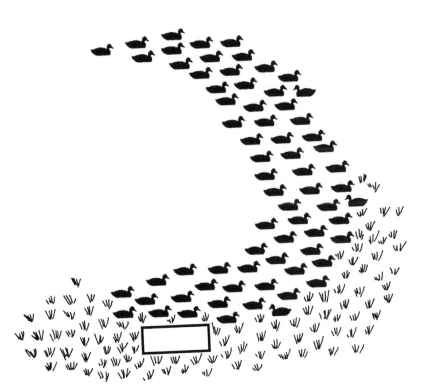

The big marsh set utilizes larger numbers of decoys, often magnum. A large oval is some-times used.

head decoy anchored upstream prevent some line entanglement, but not always. Goose decoys can be used as confidence decoys, but should be placed separately from the duck decoys. It's harder to create a pocket in this situation, but you should be positioned toward the back of the rig.

River-set decoys should, if at all possible, be positioned out of the main current because that's where the ducks will want to land. As the season progresses and lakes, ponds, and marshes freeze over, these river pockets can become even more productive.

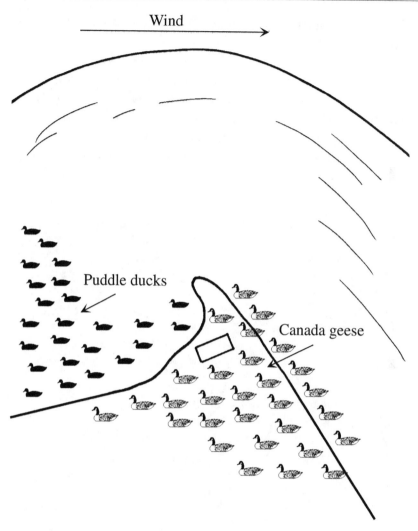

Wind

Puddle ducks

Canada geese

River sets often use a J-pattern, the length of the long arm depending on the current.

FLOODED TIMBER SETS

Some of the most exciting and traditional waterfowling occurs in flooded timber. Flooded oak, pecan, cypress, and hickory trees provide a gourmet feast puddle ducks such as mallards and wood ducks simply can't resist. Quite often ducks, once committed to a flooded timber set, will drop in like leaves without the frustrating and agonizing circling often experienced in open water.

Blinds may or may not be used in timber hunting. Often simply standing by a tree is all that's needed for concealment. You also don't really need a lot of decoys. A half dozen is usually more than adequate. Water motion is actually more important than numbers of decoys, and this can be created simply by moving your foot, or with wiggler motion-type floating decoys. Wood ducks work well as confidence decoys, and their colorful plumage makes them easy to see.

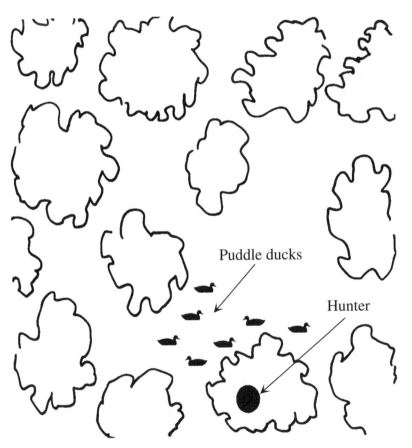

Flooded timber sets are a fairly loose-appearing set with few decoys, except in highly hunted areas; then more decoys are required.

As the season progresses and the tree canopy becomes more open, increase the number of decoys. The sets should still be small, only two to three dozen decoys at most.

FLOODED GRAIN FIELD SETS

Flooded fields of corn, soybeans, and harvested rice offer some of the most exciting waterfowling to many gunners in grain belt country. I've had the opportunity to hunt the rice fields of Arkansas a number of times, including one hunt with Governor Huckabee. The experience was pure Arkansas duck hunting, maybe some of the best in the world.

The sets are usually made in shallow-water situations created in the flooded rice fields, often in conjunction with sunken pit blinds. One such blind I hunted with Tom Matthews and the Mossy Oak crew had eight hunters in one blind, and we all took limits with only one hen mallard in the bunch. And that's

Flooded rice and other grain sets often involve vast numbers of decoys to compete with other hunters. A common set is a C or oval with open pockets on two sides of the blind to provide more versatility.

typical of the hunting opportunities. These hunting spots are scattered over vast fields, with lots of competition from other gunners. Typically, in this case vast numbers of decoys are often used. "We put out 2,000 to 3,000 decoys," said Tom Matthews. In this case the decoys are often scattered over a very wide area, with just a small pocket in front of the blind. One blind we hunted from had a pocket in front and back and a swiveling top so you could hunt either side depending on the wind.

I've also hunted similar situations, including one on a private club near Kansas City, Missouri, that had a flooded milo field, with the water just below the tops of the grain heads. You couldn't keep the ducks out of that field, and only a half dozen decoys were needed.

Another flooded grain field situation I hunted was on a private lease just outside the Squaw Creek National Wildlife Refuge. With 40 acres of flooded corn, a blind in the center, and decoys surrounding it on all sides, the shooting was great. About eight dozen decoys were used to pull in the ducks, with a small landing pocket in front of the blind.

DRY-LAND FIELD SETS

Although many people don't think of ducks as "land" birds, freshly harvested grain fields with lots of waste grain on the ground are great duck magnets. In some cases, grain fields are planted around sloughs to attract ducks, with permanent blinds located along the edges of the slough. Opportunistic hunters can also set up in freshly harvested grain fields that are being used temporarily by ducks. This is basically a scout and locate situation.

Dry-land duck gunning requires field decoys. These can consist of shells, silhouettes, or specialized decoys such as the Flambeau Pontoon Perimeter models. A typical set is in a J- or hook shape with the gunners or blind in the middle of the lower part of the set. Best shooting is with the wind crosswise of the set. A separate group of Canada geese makes an excellent confidence addition. The Flambeau full-bodied mallard Enticer models are also excellent confidence decoys. Good concealment is important in this type of set. A number of decoys are normally used—we often use 300 to 400.

Wind

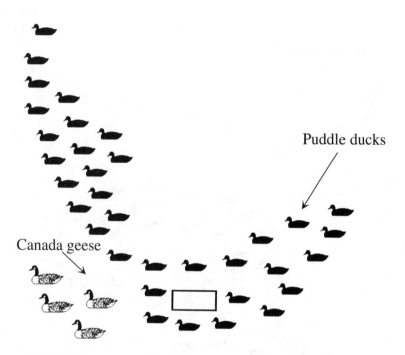

Dry-land field sets require lots of duck decoys. The typical pattern is a J or V. Goose decoys to the side add realism and act as confidence decoys.

RESERVOIR OR LAKE LAND SETS

Many of the larger reservoirs and natural lakes across the country produce extremely good public land for waterfowling. This can be for puddle ducks, divers, or sea ducks. Some of the best decoying locations are long points that extend out into the lake or reservoir. Although crossing wind is good, the best situation is with the wind to your back. On a crossing wind in open water, ducks may land outside your spread. With the wind to your back, they tend to land closer in the pocket. A V- or C-spread works well for this, and it's a good idea to combine puddle and diver duck decoys. Position the puddle ducks close to shore and as the main set, then run an attractor string of divers out into the lake. If ducks are landing outside the pocket, move the divers in more. A half dozen Canada goose decoys placed on the land act as confidence decoys. Large numbers of decoys are often necessary for this tactic, both puddlers and divers. Three hundred or 400 is not uncommon on the reservoirs we hunt. The decoys should also be large, or magnum sized.

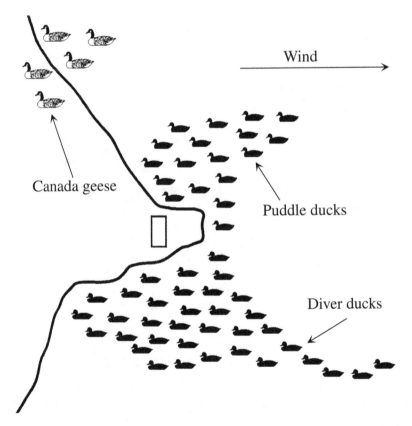

Reservoir or lake land sets are often created on points or cuts in coves. A V is the best shape for cuts, with a C on points. Vary the species; goose and other confidence decoys are important.

OPEN-WATER DIVER SETS

Open-water gunning for diver ducks is one of the most challenging and exciting forms of waterfowling. Huge rafts of divers often collect on the open waters of lakes, bays, or reservoirs. Shooting is from a stake blind, floating blind, or low-profile boat. The decoys are normally rigged around the blind in a J- or hooked set. A leader line of decoys runs for 100 yards or so out away from the set. The throat or open part of the hook should face with the wind.

Open-water gunning of divers requires large numbers of decoys to create the semblance of rafting ducks. A couple of hundred decoys are often needed to create a productive set. Chapter 17 provides more detailed information on diver and sea duck hunting.

Diver ducks

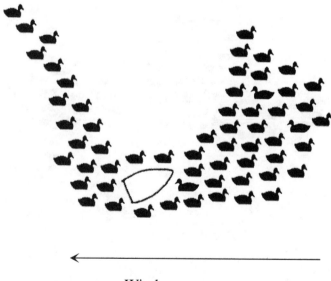

Wind

Open-water diver sets are challenging. Large numbers of decoys are needed. A J- or hooked set is the most common, with the blind in the center of the lower arm of the J and a string of gang-rigged decoys leading out into open water.

OPEN-WATER SETS, MIXED SPECIES

Many lakes and reservoirs hold a wide variety of waterfowl species, and open-water sets in these areas can be productive for divers as well as puddle ducks. Decoys for both species should be used. Create two separate sets, one on each side of the blind or boat. A C- or J-pattern is used for each species, actually creating a giant S-set. Diver ducks readily fly over decoys, often buzzing quite close. Puddle ducks, however, rarely fly over decoys. The secret is to create the landing pocket with the wind so the puddle ducks have plenty of open space to drop in, while still allowing a close-in landing zone for the divers.

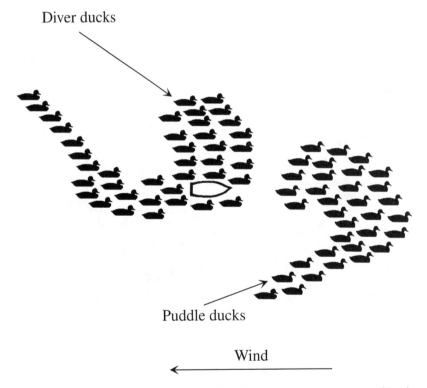

Diver ducks

Puddle ducks

Wind

The open water of reservoirs and big lakes offers the opportunity to create combination sets with both diver and puddle ducks. The species must be positioned separately and a double J or S is often used.

Diver decoys should be used for the majority of the set, and they can be placed fairly tight together since they have a tendency to raft close together. Again, a long attractor string can be used to bring divers into the set, and you'll need lots of decoys.

PRO TIPS

"You need to create a shooting zone," said Chris Paradise of Flambeau. "You build a decoy spread that allows you the cleanest possible shot, where the birds are within range of your shots. Always place your decoys by the wind. Birds always land and take off into the wind. So if you place decoys upwind and you place decoys downwind, you create a void in the middle. In that area is where you typically place your blind, whether on land or water—somewhere in that void. That does two things: One, you put the majority of your decoys up in the upwind portion of the spread. The birds automatically want to get to that position, but they need a landing zone. You also have some decoys

"Create a shooting zone with your decoys," said Chris Paradise. "Place a marker decoy at 35 yards so you can determine the shooting range."

trailing downwind. Creating a landing zone where you know where they are going to come to makes for more productive and exciting hunting.

"There's another tactic in shooting mallards that is real popular with our full-bodied Mallard Enticers. You can use them in a number of ways, on land, around water, or on ice. They are especially effective on ice. If you have a spot of open water in the ice, on a river, pond, or whatever, place these up on the ice. Usually the holes in the water in ice situations aren't very big. When you get a lot of birds coming to those holes in the ice, if there is not enough room for them to land they'll move somewhere else. If you place a bunch of the Enticer full bodies up on the ice and sprinkle a few standard decoys in the open hole, you've created a whole new realism look that the birds aren't used to seeing."

"Depending on where I'm hunting, I use more or less decoys," said Avery pro staffer Jarad Perkins. "It just depends on each scenario for me to know how many and how I'm going to set my decoys up. Late in the season, hunting a field, set your decoys downwind. That way the birds have to come across you. If they are staying shy, especially later in the season, a trick I like to

"In warm weather spread out your decoys," said Kelley Powers. "In cold weather group them tighter."

use is set my decoys downwind. I put them where those birds are going to have to come through me first if they light into the wind to get to those decoys. That way if the birds are staying shy of the decoys, you might do better."

"Where I'm from guys put out a lot of big spreads," said Kelly Powers. "They average 500, 600, up to 1,000 duck and goose decoy combinations. I've done studies from an airplane, and if a person is hunting a 1,000-acre reservoir and they have 1,000 decoys, the surface area they cover when they set out their decoys is really tight. In a natural situation, if you have 1,000 ducks, 1,000 geese, or 1,000 duck-and-goose combos sitting on the reservoir, they're going to be sitting really spread out, or are going to be in little groups here and there. But a lot of people really bunch their decoys up too tight to look natural from the air.

"I really feel when times get tough, when you get into the third or fourth week of the season, a lot of birds pinpoint that and they become wary. It's one of those things. People scout out decoys and cut back on their numbers. I don't think they necessarily need to cut back on their numbers; it's just because a lot of people have a lot of decoys and they are not really looking at the big picture. They don't want to put their decoys out very far because of the distance. When you look from the air you can really see it—it's like the blind is a bull's-eye. If you want to hunt over 2,000 decoys and really spread them out, you can be really effective getting ducks to land in the water. They may land 150 or 200 yards out where those decoys are, but you're going to get them to work your spread, if everything else is right.

"Then there's the weather. They are going to sit spread out a lot more in warm weather. If it's cold weather they are going to sit tighter—that's just the nature of the birds, which you learn when you watch all the things that they do in all the conditions."

8

GOOSE DECOY SETS

It was cold and gray with a stiff north wind blowing and a faint sliver of dawn showing when we finally crawled into the warmth of our concrete goose pit located in the center of a cornfield. We had spent nearly an hour assembling and arranging over 400 Canada goose decoys, and my hands were stiff with the cold. Cups of steaming-hot coffee were poured, and we sat and warmed ourselves with the coffee and thoughts of the excitement to come. High overhead in the mysterious darkness we heard geese milling and calling to those on the ground, resting in rafts of thousands out on the nearby refuge lake.

As the light streak of dawn began to widen, we saw the flights of Canada geese passing around and over us. I noted two of our silhouettes had tipped over slightly and I quickly climbed out of the blind, sprinted to them, and staked them upright. Back in the blind I anxiously checked my watch, waiting for the official shooting time to begin. Even the most grizzled veteran goose hunters would have come unglued at the sight before us. The sky above us was filled with thousands of geese when we finally agreed it was time to shoot. We heard the booming of guns from blinds on other portions of the public hunting areas, but for the first few minutes of legal shooting time the flights bypassed us as they headed out from the safety of the refuge and into the surrounding grain fields to feed.

Suddenly a flight was coming in low and passing close to our blind. I picked up my goose call and began calling to the flock. Knowing the wary geese were getting somewhat call-shy from the pressure, I gave a few K-LUKS to keep them interested, but otherwise kept quiet. I glanced at our decoys out of the corner of my eye. Were they good enough to compete with the other hunters? Would the geese come in or flare? It was up to the decoy spread now. We had spent a great deal of time accumulating the large number of high-quality decoys and I hoped our spread would attract the wary birds.

Slowly the flight worked in closer, seemingly moving away at times, then back as the line of geese wavered in flight: 150 yards, 100 yards, 50 yards. Then the huge webbed feet of the leaders of the flock spread out wide in front to take the shock of their landing.

"Now," I yelled. On the far left side of the blind, I took the second goose back on my side. The Beretta boomed and I saw the bird buck slightly. My second shot hit hard, and the goose dropped the few remaining feet to the ground. I quickly swung on the first bird, now departing fast, and, with a lucky shot, doubled and brought him down with a loud thump.

We quickly ran to retrieve our geese. Before we were situated back in the blind, another group headed toward us. Excitedly we all started calling to them. They turned away and we couldn't persuade them to come back.

Another flight out in front of us banked and started making a slow circle to bring them in over our decoys. We had calmed down by now and gave only a few K-LUKS. Maddeningly slow they came in to the decoys, long necks waving back and forth as they minutely examined the scene below them. Then they were in and we rose to shoot.

Goose hunting provides some of the most thrilling and challenging of waterfowling. The birds are big, smart, and hard to decoy and call, especially local geese that know their territory like you and I know our living rooms.

Goose hunting consists of hunting migrating and resident Canada geese, whitefronted or specklebelly geese, and snow and blue geese. Each requires somewhat different tactics and, naturally, different decoys.

Decoying Canada geese, whether on land or water, requires a lot of decoys, and usually a lot of work.

Geese also don't like to land over their brethren, and must land into the wind. Basic decoy set patterns are used, with the V the most common.

As with ducks, geese do not like to land in over other geese, and they must also land and take off into the wind. Different patterns of decoy sets can be used, including the C-, J-, or, more commonly, V-shape. Regardless of the pattern, like ducks, you have to be where the geese want to be.

CANADA GOOSE FIELD SETS

Field sets are commonly used when geese are feeding in waste grain fields, wheat fields, or other land situations. As with most goose decoying situations, you'll need a large number of decoys. Two to three dozen is considered the minimum, with larger numbers required for hard-hunted areas. It's not unusual to use 300 to 400 decoys for a feeding field set. Use only the best, most realistic decoys available and place them in a realistic feeding pattern, with the majority of

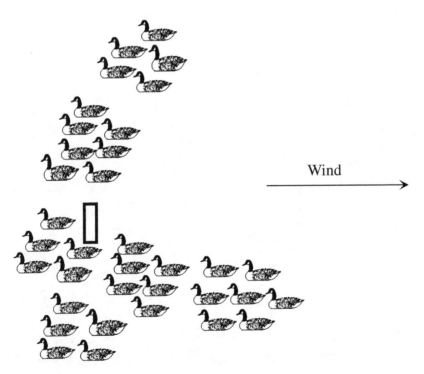

As Canada geese often congregate in family groups, many gunners like to create their spreads of family groups, with the blind in the center of the V.

the birds feeding into the wind and only a handful of alert or upright heads. Make sure the set is made according to the wind direction.

Most gunners prefer to set the geese in family groups of 10 to 12 decoys, leaving some space between the groups, as this is the manner in which Canada geese tend to group and feed. Then create a pocket or V-shape set as a landing zone with the blind or hunters in the center of the V. Make sure the set is away from fences or other obstacles. If suspicious of anything, Canada geese will warily circle just out of range. Field mallard decoys can also be set off to one side to act as confidence decoys. To increase realism, add a half dozen extremely realistic, full-bodied decoys out away from the main spread with a half dozen or so strung out between the small family group and the main spread. This gives the appearance of a family group that has just joined the flock and is walking in to feed.

Any number of motion decoys can be used to help attract distant geese. These include kite and wind-sock styles. Flagging to get the attention of distant geese is also extremely productive.

CANADA GOOSE WATER SETS

The larger reservoirs and lakes offer the excitement of gunning for geese over water. In many instances water sets may be more productive than field sets because geese roost on the water at night, leave early in the morning for the feed fields, then begin to filter back to their water resting areas through the middle of the day. Usually the geese leave the water in small groups, and the smaller groups are easier to decoy and have a tendency to come into a water set with less circling and hesitation. The sets can be made just as for ducks, with a C, J, or V. The pocket of a V-set is quite commonly used, with the blind or hunters positioned in the center of the set. If hunting from land, a few "loafers" placed on the shore will help create a relaxed look to the set. Again, duck decoys, both floaters and field style, can be used to create more confidence, as can mixing in coot decoys and a great blue heron decoy.

The good part about water sets is they usually don't require as many decoys. You're primarily decoying family groups, and that's how the decoys should be set. Position four or five here, a dozen there, maybe another six or eight in another grouping. In high-pressured areas, you're still looking at three to four dozen decoys. In this case, the bigger, long-distance attractors are the

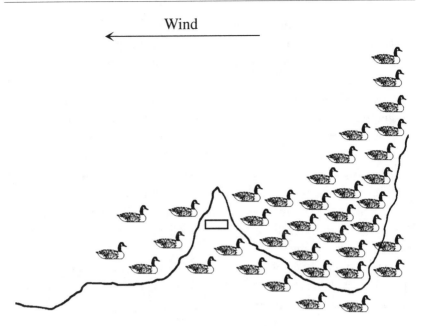

A C or V is often used for Canada water sets, depending on blind and wind directions. Floaters and land decoys should all be used.

best choice. Always use the most realistic Canada goose decoys you can afford, either floaters or full-bodied land models.

Geese also like to frequent rivers and streams. A gang set of Canada geese on a river or stream can be extremely effective at times.

SNOW AND BLUE GOOSE SETS

Almost anyone interested in waterfowling these days knows the problems with the huge populations of snow and blue geese. One of the problems is they're extremely hard to decoy—at times. At other times it seems they're idiots! The main reason for the difficulty is the vast size of the flocks. Several hundred or even several thousand birds may be in a single flock. It takes a lot of decoys and work to attract the attention of a flock that size. Two hundred to 500 decoys are probably the least you can get by with, with

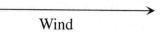

Wind

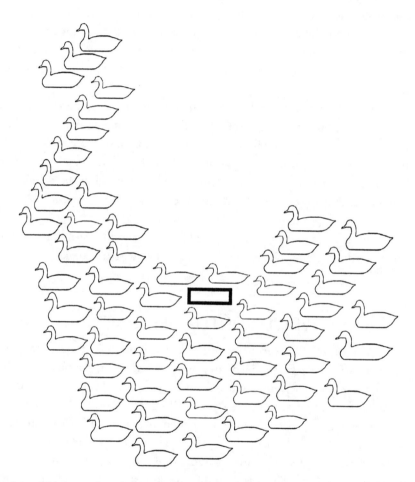

Snows and blues require enormous sets. A V-pattern, with the blind in the center, is the most common. Canada goose decoys can be set off to the side as confidence decoys.

2,000 to 3,000 not an unusual number in some locales and situations. In earlier days white diapers were often used. White plastic garbage bags are still being used, but with more hunting pressure and more wary geese, a more realistic set with better decoys is often required. Shell decoys are the best choice, and I've found the Feather Flex foam shells to be excellent for the purpose. They're lightweight and easy to set out. Silhouette decoys may be used to help fill out the set. The Texas Rag Spread is another excellent way to add to the set. It can be draped over stubble or made into a wind sock.

As snow geese can quickly demolish a feeding field, they are constantly on the move. Follow a flock and watch from a distance to determine their feeding field, then dig a pit blind and be in position in the center of the field before daylight the next morning with all the decoys you can afford around you. The most common set is a V, or oval, with the blind in the center and wings extending to the side. If you want to add Canada goose decoys as confidence decoys, position them off to the side. With all the commotion of the huge numbers of geese in a snow or blue flock, motion is important. But don't overdo it. Once you get their attention, they wise up quickly.

WHITEFRONTED GEESE SETS

Whitefronted or specklebelly geese are hunted in much the same manner as Canada geese. They are, however, normally found in smaller flocks than snows and blues, and smaller decoy sets will usually bring them in. Whitefronted geese will often come into decoy sets of other species. If whitefronted geese are in the area, it's a good idea to mix a few whitefronted decoys in with your Canada or snow and blue set. Specklebellies have a very disconcerting habit of circling and circling warily just out of range for long periods of time. The sets should be made just as for Canada geese and snows or blues.

COMBINATION GOOSE SETS

Combination sets can be used in areas that have a combination of goose species, and are a good way of creating a bigger spread. The spread should

Wind

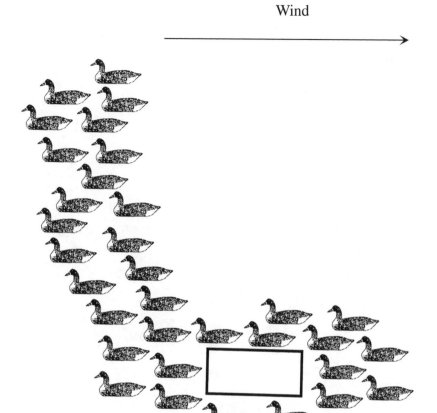

Whitefronted or specklebelly geese sets are made more like Canada sets, as they typically travel in smaller groups than snows and blues.

again be in the typical C-shape with the wind either crosswise or to your back. The main set should be snows and blues with a secondary and separate Canada set off to one side. Whitefronted geese can be intermingled throughout the set. Add field mallards to the set for confidence decoys.

PRO TIPS

"Decoys are really important when hunting geese," said Fred Zink. "Especially getting the right decoys and the right number of decoys. I have to

Wind

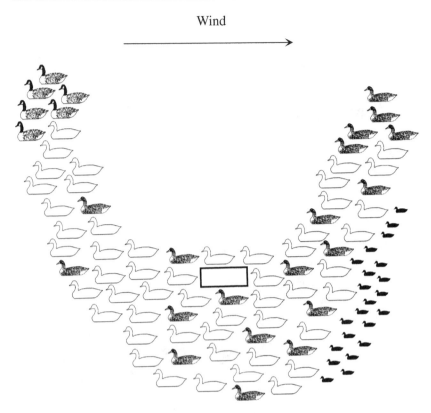

Combination sets can be used to bring in snows and blues as well as Canada geese. The two species should be set apart. Specklebelly decoys can be scattered throughout the set.

say, the biggest part of decoying Canada geese, day in and day out, with dumb geese and smart geese, is having a decoy spread that is realistic to what the geese are doing. For instance, is it real warm out or is it midseason or have the geese have been shot at a lot? You have to match the spread to each situation. For instance, you have a big spread of shell decoys and you're doing something wrong; the birds just aren't working. A shell decoy imitates a goose lying down, and in that warm-weather condition, a goose is not going to lie down. You're throwing something at him that is very, very fake, unnatural. It works for a while until he figures it out. That warm-weather condition would be a good time to use a full body or a silhouette. As the year goes on and it gets cold, then the geese will lie down, even to feed. A shell decoy is very effective at that time. It is also the time when the geese have been shot at by people using full-bodied and silhouette decoys for some time. So going to a shell decoy late can be very good.

"How you set your decoys is also important. If it is warm and mild you should scatter your decoys in small family groups. In cold weather, group them closer together. Then use a real good-looking full-bodied goose decoy, such as those from Higdon, to make the set as realistic as possible."

"Really good decoys, such as those from Higdon, are important," said Fred Zink. "And the set must be realistic as to what the geese are doing at that time."

9

COMBINATION SETS

The flight came in fast, without hesitation, flashing white, blue, green, and brown. My hunting buddy Jack Nelson raised his shotgun above the tiny tree-limb blind stuck in the mud bank.

"Don't shoot, they're shovelers," I yelled.

"Love to eat shovelers," came the terse reply as his automatic, along with several others in the blind, began to boom. It was over in moments. When we retrieved the colorful birds and started counting points, Jack and I were limited out, but a couple of our buddies in the blind were still a bird short.

They didn't have long to wait. Almost before we were settled again in the blind, a half dozen green-wing teal buzzed us. After a flurry of shots, one of the tiny birds floated on the water.

"One more to go," encouraged Jack to our hunting partners. A half hour later came the buzzing sound of bluebills, and a suicidal bird made a dive-bombing strafing run right over the top of the blind. He was added to the pile of birds, ending one of the most unusual duck hunting days I've experienced.

Hunting three hours, opening day on Truman Reservoir in central Missouri, we had collected a total mixed bag of ducks, including mallards, blue-wing and green-wing teal, a wood duck, shovelers, gadwall, pintails, bluebills, and a couple of widgeon. A few weeks later we added to the variety with several Canada geese, a goldeneye, and a single specklebelly. The hunt took place several years ago during the "point system regulations."

Probably the main reason for our unusual success was simply because there was a large variety of waterfowl species in the area. This can be typical of opening day in some parts of the country. During the early part of the season, in many parts of the country, mallards, the most common duck, may be in short supply, while the early migrators such as teal may be more abundant. But in other parts of the country, the species variety becomes greater as the season progresses and diver ducks are added to the pot. Then the goose seasons kick in and you have even more alternatives.

One of the reasons for the success described, however, is that we were ready for anything, not only in calls but in decoys as well. In multispecies areas, I don't like to leave anyone out. Granted, most species will readily decoy

Waterfowlers lucky enough to live in parts of the country with a variety of waterfowl can increase their chances for success by using combination sets, combining different species of duck and goose decoys.

to mallard decoys, but I use the other species decoys not only as confidence decoys for the mallards, but also as attractors for the different species. I do, however, choose the decoys to match the prevalent species in the area.

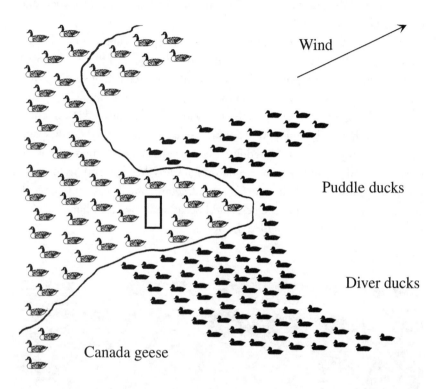

Reservoir Land Set

Small potholes, marshes, ponds, and reservoir attract numerous puddle ducks and resident geese. Use a combination of puddlers with geese off to the side and on land. Vary the number of the decoys according to the size of the water hunted.

SMALL-WATER POTHOLES AND PONDS

Small potholes and ponds are primarily a puddle duck situation, but again the species can vary. The primary decoy species will be mallards, with a mix of other species. In almost all situations the separate species decoys should be set slightly apart. Early in the season I like to add almost as many green-wing teal as mallards. I place the mallards out in the deeper water and the teal extremely close to shore, as they prefer the more shallow, mudflat types of water. If goose season is open, I add two pairs of Canada honkers off to one side as well. If the pothole is in flooded timber, I add a half dozen wood duck decoys, half drakes, half hens.

As the season progresses, I add the different species at the times they typically migrate through the area. By midseason I've changed the teal decoys to pintails, widgeon, and gadwalls. I especially like to place five or six gadwalls to create the top of the C or a pocket on the outside edge of my decoys. And I group them tightly because that's the way gadwalls act. They're kind of antisocial to the other birds, and tend to land just outside the decoys if decoy species such as mallards are used. But adding the gadwalls can draw them closer into the pocket and also entices wary mallards. I always add a few pintails to the set, not only because I feel their colors are an attractant, but also as confidence decoys for mallards and other species. And I occasionally get the chance to shoot some bull pintails with the added decoys.

Adding pintails to mallard sets can create confidence. Or add in gadwalls if they are a common species in the area.

As the season progresses, I like to add more Canada goose decoys and cut back on the ducks. The big honkers bring in the ducks and also the geese. I still keep a variety of puddle duck species in the set, but not teal. The basic set is a C-shape with the different species set within the pattern but apart from each other.

OPEN-WATER SETS

The opportunities for more species increases with open-water sets on reservoirs and big lakes. As with the hunt described earlier, large reservoirs are mixed-bag hunting. You really don't know what you'll find coming into your spread each day. I remember a ruddy duck that visited our blind for three weeks out of a season while we were hammering any number of puddle and diver ducks along with some geese. The little stiff-tailed bird swam in and around our decoys, in front of our blind, his tail at full mast, almost as if taunting us to shoot him. We didn't, and he offered amusement for many hours.

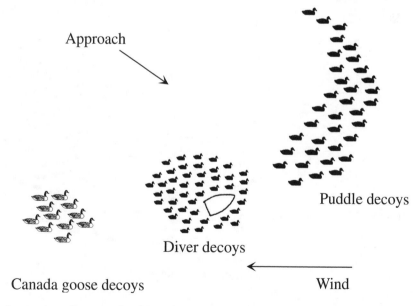

Approach

Puddle decoys

Diver decoys

Canada goose decoys

Wind

Open-water sets can consist of just about anything you can imagine, including a variety of puddle ducks, diver ducks, and geese. Keep the puddle duck and goose decoys separate.

The season tally from that same blind, which was a shore blind situated on a major reservoir, resulted in green-wing and blue-wing teal, mallards, pintails, gadwalls, widgeon, bluebills, redheads, two canvasbacks, a number of goldeneye and buffleheads, and we watched a hooded merganser for a week. We also killed Canada and snow and blue geese out of the same blind.

Again part of the reason for the multispecies success was a multispecies combination set. The set was in a J-shape with mallard decoys the primary species, set on the right-hand side, with the wind primarily from the right. On the outside edge of the mallard set was a diver spread of canvasbacks with a mother line leading about 100 yards offshore. A few gadwalls and pintails made up a small segment of the left-hand side. Then a bit farther out a mixed

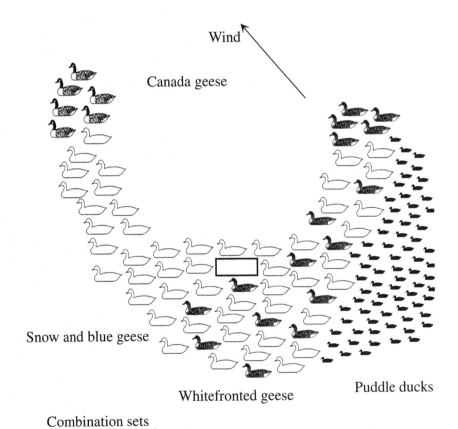

Wind

Canada geese

Snow and blue geese

Whitefronted geese

Puddle ducks

Combination sets

Field sets with both ducks and all goose species can be extremely productive at times.

bag of divers, grouped according to species, completed the left-hand side for the ducks. A half dozen full-bodied Canada geese were scattered on shore, with two dozen placed just on the inside of the divers to the left side. As the season progressed and the species varied, we continued to add and subtract the decoy species.

PRO TIPS

"Where we hunt in northwest Tennessee—and this applies anywhere from Canada to Texas—anytime when we have some severe weather and it drives the Canada geese down to us, we set up a combo of decoys," said expert goose hunter Tommy Akin. "We're using both mallards or puddle ducks and Canada floaters as well as Canada full bodies. The temperature at the time we are hunting determines how tight we set the decoys together. If it is sort of mild, we scatter both the floater and full-bodied goose decoys out much, much more than we do when it's bitter, bitter cold conditions. When it's bitter cold, with ice, we pick up most of our mallard decoys, bust a hole out in front of our

Use Canada floaters as full sets for ducks when the weather gets bitter.

pit, and put the full-bodied goose decoys real, real tight on the ice around the open water. Then we put a few Canada geese floaters in the open water itself. We pretty well take the duck decoys out of the picture at that time because we don't need them.

"If it's not really bitter, we use big spreads of both ducks and Canada geese. We put out anywhere from 300 to 500 duck decoys, anywhere from 50 to 200 goose floaters, and another 75 to 150 full-bodied goose decoys. We separate the decoys; I don't mix them together. We hunt really shallow water. I put the Canada geese by themselves; I also mix the stand-up geese in with the floaters. If you go to a refuge and watch the birds, you'll see ducks and geese are naturally separated, so that's what we do.

"When field hunting in Canada, we hunt snow geese, Canada geese, and mallards all at the same time. We put snow geese in one set and we put the Canada geese off by themselves, in front, left or right, or behind us. We do not mix them together either. We put out very few duck decoys. We hunt a dry pit, and the goose decoys pull in the ducks. The ducks are coming to the feeding field."

"Combination spreads are tricky," said Chris Paradise with Flambeau. "I don't know what it is, but ducks do not like to land over geese. Usually I'm not primarily going after geese, so I set the goose decoys to one side, typically upwind of the ducks, so when the ducks come in downwind they don't have to go over the geese. I put all the geese in one end and all the ducks in the other end.

"I do the same thing on water—I don't intermingle the decoys. If you're going after ducks—they're your targeted species—make sure you position the decoys so the ducks don't have to fly over the geese."

10

DECOY
MAINTENANCE

Maintaining decoys is a major part of waterfowling. And if you have a large number of blocks, the work can get quite involved. The amount and type of maintenance depends on the type of decoys, as well as what they are made of. At the end of the waterfowl season I get lazy and simply store all the dekes in the barn, without any thought to repair. Then, about a month before the next waterfowl season begins, I start thinking about the upcoming season, drag all my decoys out, and do the maintenance and repair.

STORING DECOYS

Proper storage is an important factor in how much maintenance is required. Don't just throw the decoys in a corner of the garage where they'll eventually get other items thrown on top of them. Racks or shelves constructed along a garage or shed wall provide the best storage conditions.

"A lot of people take their decoys, put them in a bag and throw them in the attic or the top of their garage," said Chris Paradise of Flambeau. "Then

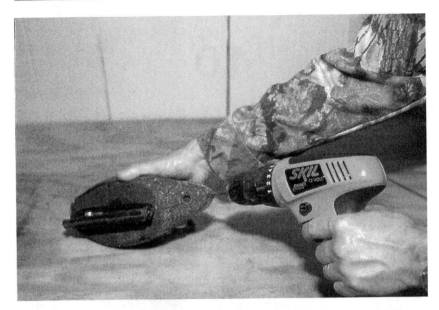

Waterfowl decoys require maintenance—it's a fact of life. But that's not necessarily bad. Repairing decoys can bring memories of past seasons or dreams for the upcoming season.

they complain, 'The paint is coming off my decoys, what's the matter.' The problem is the decoys have been sitting up in an attic in 120-degree temperatures all summer. This temperature change starts to break down the paint on the plastic. The heat also expands or blows them up a little bit and deforms the decoys. Decoys should be stored in well-ventilated areas, and not in damp or extremely hot, dry areas."

The decoys should also be stored out of direct sunlight, as the ultraviolet rays can damage the paint and plastic. Pests such as rats, mice, or squirrels also tend to chew on some types of decoys, the foam ones in particular. Having the decoys in bags hung up on the wall can solve this problem as well.

CLEANING

Decoys become algae covered and discolored from being left in the water. They're also typically exposed to a lot of mud, sand, and other debris. A thorough cleaning is the first step. You can then determine any damage that needs to be repaired. Mud, particularly the sticky, "gumbo" type often found in waterfowling areas, sticks to decoys like glue. It is easiest to remove while

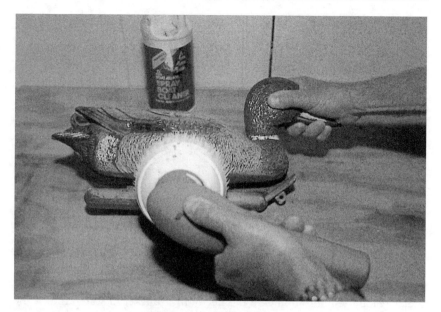

It's suggested to thoroughly clean decoys at the end of the season—it's easier then. I never do, but by then it's hard to get the dried mud and grime off. Marine boat cleaners do a good job.

still fairly fresh; you may wish to clean your decoys at the end of the season rather than waiting until the next season when the grime has hardened in place like concrete. A marine algaecide used to clean boat bottoms can be used to remove water scum and dried algae. Then use a marine soap and water to scrub the grime and mud from the decoys. A stiff-bristle scrub brush may be necessary to get all the hardened material off. A good pressure washer can also be used, but watch that your don't "blow" the paint off as well. Then hang the decoys in a dry place out of the sun to dry thoroughly. A light coating of Armor-All will keep the decoys clean and bright looking.

If the decoys are chalked or dull looking, use a bit of marine fiberglass cleaner to reduce the chalking and brighten the colors.

INSPECTION

When it's time to repair your blocks, take them all out of their bags or off the racks and inspect them thoroughly. Then start separate piles of the "wounded" dekes. Those missing strings or anchors should be placed in one pile. Those with holes or cracks in the seam should be placed in one area and those with bad or missing paint placed in another pile.

REPAIRING HOLES AND CRACKS

People tend to shoot their decoys. Ice and hard wear can split the seams, cause cracks, and do other damage in hollow plastic or hard rubber decoys. In some cases the keel may also come off. If the decoy is so badly damaged it can't be used as a floater, I use a sharp knife on hard rubber and a hacksaw on plastic decoys to cut the bottom completely away, creating a "field" decoy. You can also add a wooden bottom to help the decoy hold its shape and provide more stability and weight.

Shot and other small holes as well as minor cracks can be sealed with marine silicone caulk. The first step is to locate the holes and cracks if they aren't readily visible. Submerge the decoy in a bucket of water and, if the

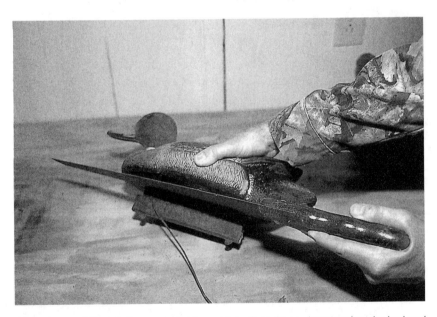

Badly damaged floater decoys can be turned into field decoys by removing the keel and bottom.

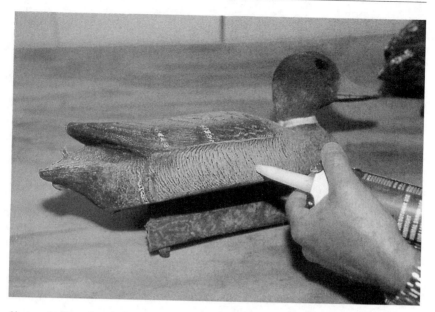

Shot and other minor holes and cracks can be repaired with marine silicone.

decoy is rubber, squeeze it. If the decoy is hard plastic, simply shake it. Then note where the water comes out. Use a drill bit in a portable electric drill to enlarge the hole slightly and to "mark" it. Drill a small hole in the tip of the tail and place the decoy tail-down on a rack or hang it from a nail on the wall, tail-down. Leave the decoy in this position for several days to allow all the water to drain out.

Apply the marine silicone sealant to the holes and cracks, forcing it down into the holes and cracks. Use a screwdriver blade or small putty knife to smooth the sealant around the hole or crack and allow the decoy to dry the amount of time suggested by the manufacturer of the marine silicone sealant, which is usually overnight.

"My fix-it plan for decoys with shot holes is to buy a can of spray-foam insulation," said Chris Paradise. "Drill a hole in the top of the decoy and drill a hole in the bottom in the opposite end. Spray one- or two-second sprits in the bottom hole. The foam fills the decoy and flows out the hole in the top of the head. Now your decoy is fixed for life. You can't sink it. You can shoot it a hundred times and it will still be fine."

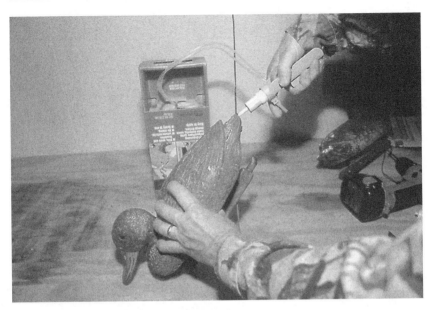

"A great way of repairing shot damaged floaters is to fill them with spray-foam insulation," suggested Chris Paradise.

REPAINTING

Over time even the best of decoys begin to lose their paint, becoming dull or less realistic looking. Repainting decoys is not particularly hard. Ordinary latex, acrylic, or oil-based paints may be used on plastic, hard rubber, wood, or cork decoys. These paints can be purchased at your local hardware store, or they can be paints especially formulated for decoys. For a number of years I've used Herter's World Famous Decoy Paints. The finish is dull, yet waterproof and durable and, most important, the colors are mixed exactly as they should be to match the different waterfowl species. The Herter's paint will work well on balsa, wood, cork, plastic, and hard rubber. The paints are available separately, or in kits with just the right amounts of each color to match the pattern for specific species. The kits available include mallard, black duck, bluebill, canvasback, pintail, redhead, coot, snow goose, Canada goose, goldeneye, black brant, blue goose, specklebelly, wood duck, green-wing teal, blue-wing teal, bufflehead, baldpate, scoter, oldsquaw, eider, ringbill, and gadwall. Each kit comes with enough paint for two dozen life-sized duck decoys, six goose decoys or six silhouettes, and all the instructions.

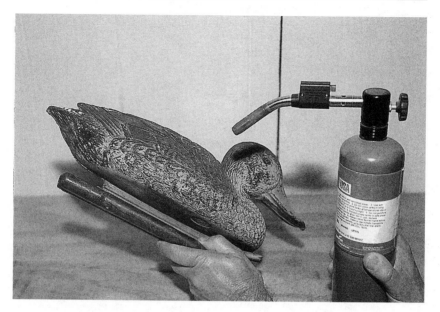

Before painting, all grime and old paint must be removed.

Old-time waterfowlers often painted two sets of blocks. One set was painted with fairly dull colors to match the plumage of the early migrating birds. The other was painted with bright plumage to match the later-migrating birds and also to provide more attention getting for late-season ducks.

"The first thing you need to do if repainting decoys is what we call flame purification," said Paradise. "Take a blowtorch and go over the entire bird, not so close that you melt it, but just to burn off some of the dirt and impurities in the old paint. You can then use a water-based paint, like latex, or an oil-based paint. The oil-based paint will hold up a little longer, but there is the chance it will bubble up on the plastic. I also suggest a water-based paint because it breathes."

The old scaling or loosened paint can also be removed with a stiff-bristle brush.

Regardless of the paint chosen, it should be a flat or matte finish rather than shiny or reflective. If using an oil-based paint, use turpentine or other "dryers" to flatten the sheen. If the decoys take on a sheen, use kitchen scouring powder to help cut the shine. A favorite tactic of the old-timers was to paint their decoys, then sit the decoys in the sun for a few weeks to age.

Patterns don't have to be "decoy art" realistic, but should match the pattern color markings of the species.

Before applying the paint, the decoy should be primed. This is best done with a latex primer, or you can use Zinsser Shellac Sealer & Finish. It's available in a spray can and is designed to function as an undercoating or primer for hard-to-stick surfaces.

The pattern you apply to such details as feathering can be as realistic or as simplistic as you desire, or have the time and talent to do. In most instances you won't want to paint working decoys as realistic as decorative decoys. It's the color patterns rather than individual feathering that create the realism of working blocks. Magazines such as *Ducks Unlimited, Delta Waterfowl,* and birds books can all be used as "pattern" ideas to determine the colors as well as location of the colors on the different species.

If the decoy has raised feathering, the first step is to paint the underlaying, or usually the darker, paint coat. Then use a sponge dipped in a contrasting color to highlight the feathers. A small brush can also be used.

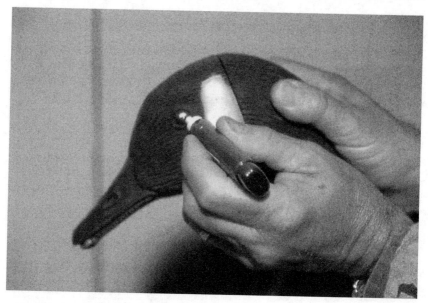

Adding a white highlight to the eye adds realism.

In areas, particularly on the head, where the colors run into each other, apply both paints wet and feather the colors together with a clean, dry brush.

I also like to add a white highlight to the eyes of decoys that don't have glass eyes.

RIGGING REPAIRS

The next step is to repair the rigging. Replace any broken or missing decoys cords and replace any lost anchors. Decoy rigging information is covered in chapter 6.

PRO TIPS

"If you waterfowl hunt with family, friends, or in a club where everybody brings decoys," said Mark Burch, "put your name on the bottom of each of your decoys with a permanent marker. Do this when you're getting your rigs

"Write your name and phone number on the bottom of the decoy," suggested Mark Burch. "Then you might get them back if they 'escape.' "

ready for the season and you will all still be friends at the end of the season. It doesn't hurt to include your phone number. I had some decoys returned, once."

11

BLINDS AND OTHER GEAR

Staying concealed is a major factor in waterfowling success, regardless of whether you're hunting big honkers in harvested grain fields, mallards in the marshes, or scaup from the shoreline of a big lake. Blinds can consist of everything from an expensive sunken concrete or metal pit blind to nothing more than a handful of rocks strategically piled on a windy lakeshore, or a few saplings, brush, and reeds placed to provide concealment. You can also make your own permanent or temporary waterfowl blinds from a wide variety of materials. My son Mark and I often use discarded wooden pallets or skids, simply wiring them together to create a "box." We then cover the blind over with natural materials consisting of marsh grass, reeds, or brush. Commercial blind materials, such as burlap or leaf-cut camouflage cloth, are often added to help break up the outline. These will usually last the season and can then be removed if hunting on public lands where blinds must be removed.

Permanent blinds range from simple wooden boxes with a roof to keep off the elements and provide concealment to extremely large and fancy models

Staying concealed is probably the single most important facet of waterfowling. A good blind that matches the terrain and vegetation is absolutely necessary. The lid slides back on this blind to conceal the hunters.

that will hold numerous hunters, their dogs, and all their gear. One such blind I hunted was with Wildlife Farms in Arkansas. The blind would hold a dozen hunters easily, had room for a stove and cooking space in one corner and "conning" towers on both ends so the guides could call the ducks and tell the hunters when to shoot.

One of the most unusual blinds I've hunted from was with Avery Outdoors on a lake near Stuttgart, Arkansas. The blind was shaped like a huge 45-degree V. Each side of the V was about 36 feet long, and the inside of the V concealed a boat. Sunk on pilings in the lake, the blind was totally covered and extremely comfortable, even with a dozen hunters. With the two sides facing somewhat different directions, it also offered a variety of shooting positions to match different wind directions.

I had the good fortune for many years to hunt with Judge Kelso of southwestern Missouri. His private waterfowl honeyhole consisted of an oxbow of a river surrounding a stand of timber. He had two blinds located in the timbered oxbow, both sunken concrete. When he flooded the oxbow each year, the

Permanent blinds can range from a simple camouflage-covered box for weather protection and concealment to an elaborate blind complete with stove, cooking space, and room for multiple hunters.

When it comes to hunter numbers and diversity, a V-shaped blind I hunted in Arkansas provided the best of both, with boat storage behind.

water level came to just about a half foot below the top of the blinds. It was an unusual feeling to be sitting below the water level. When the ducks came in—and they normally did in big numbers—the shooting was more at eye level as they started to settle in the decoys. Many of my more memorable hunts took place in that little blind. Unfortunately the land became an easement of the Corps of Engineers Truman Reservoir, and too many years of spring floods eventually killed the standing timber, ruining one of the best waterfowling spots I've ever had a chance to hunt.

A classic waterfowl blind I remember was in the Louisiana marsh, hunting with Hackberry Lodge. The blind was a simple, permanent wooden structure covered with reeds to match the existing vegetation, and my guide had been hunting the same blind for more than 20 years. Sitting in the blind, I couldn't help but think about the number of hunters and the waterfowl killed, the stories the blind could have given if only it could speak.

Gunners on famous Reelfoot Lake in Tennessee hunt out of piling blinds, or permanent wooden structures erected on pilings over the water. These range from the very simple to the very elaborate.

A blind can also be as simple as piled rocks or vegetation stuck in the mud.

Another unusual blind I hunted out of was constructed by Del Arduser on Truman Reservoir. The blind was a huge floating U-shape into which Del drove his boat. We shot out of the boat, with the big blind providing the concealment.

A number of manufactured waterfowl blinds are also available, including blinds for use on land, water, and on boats.

LAND BLINDS

Avery Outdoors may be the most innovative waterfowl manufacturer in the country, and the Avery Finisher Blind, designed by Fred Zink, is a prime example. Made of lightweight yet extremely durable steel tubing, the Finisher features a unique design with three height settings to fit any size of hunter. The low-profile blind features a Padded Boot Bag that limits shadows. The drop-down padded headrest and tapered lids offer full viewing, but instant shooting. The Finisher also comes with its exclusive Flagging Sock as well as CamoStraps for securing stalks, stubble, and brush in place. The blinds weighs only 22 pounds, and the outer cover is constructed from water-resistant, 900-denier polyester in Mossy Oak Shadow Grass. The Finisher comes in a durable carry case with adjustable shoulder strap and backpack straps. The most attractive feature is that the Finisher can be folded in half both lengthwise and widthwise into a compact 8- by 20- by 48-inch size.

A good number of manufactured blinds are available. The Avery Finisher Blind, designed by Fred Zink, is the top of the portable field blinds. It also works well for a single-person shoreline blind. (Photo courtesy Avery)

I've tested the Pro Model Eliminator Goose and Lay-Down Duck Blind from Final Approach Blinds both on ducks at our local club and on some last-minute giant Canada honkers. The Eliminator is a very high-quality blind that sets up within seconds, then collapses down flat to transport. It features a fully collapsible aluminum frame with a waterproof Cordura cover and weighs only 12 pounds. The spring-loaded lid pops open instantly for unrestricted shooting. The Pro version includes side flagging holes, 3-inch dropped headrest, and shell bag. The company also makes a Backpack Blind System for those long walks in. It's a low-profile, aluminum-frame blind that collapses flat, weighs only 6 pounds, and has a semireclined, padded seat and adjustable padded headrest. It provides hands-free carrying. The Feather Duster All-Purpose Upright Blind is perfect for hunting in standing cattails, on the edges of potholes and ponds, and in wooded areas. It weighs only 11 pounds and measures 32 by 32 by 44 inches erect and will accommodate a portable camp chair. The Final Approach Hide-A-Pooch is a great little blind for your best friend too.

Another blind I've tested extensively is the BBK Kit Blind. This high-quality blind assembles in less than five minutes, is 100 percent waterproof, and

The Final Approach Eliminator Goose and Lay-Down Duck Blind also offers excellent one-person concealment for land-based hunting. (Photo courtesy Final Approach)

The BBK blind assembles in less than five minutes and provides stand-up shooting.

is virtually airtight to keep you snug and warm. The blind has a removable roof, or you can hunt through a zip-down roof window. It comes with its own folding stool, stakes, tie-downs, and four easy-to-erect telescopic poles, and it all fits very nicely in a backpack. The blind is available as a 4-foot double, or 3-foot single model. The roof on the taller (double) model makes the blind 7 feet high with a 50-inch diameter. Weight is less than 15 pounds. The single has a 40-inch diameter with 6-foot 8-inch total height. The BBK is available in Advantage Wetlands camo or Realtree Xtra Snow Pattern.

The HayBale Blind from GooseView Industries looks like a typical large round hay bale, and duplicates the large round hay bales common to modern agriculture. Natural round hay bales are common to the landscape of ducks, geese, and cranes. The blind's heavy-duty, folding aluminum frame collapses into an easily managed, compact package for transport. When the blind is collapsed, its integral polyethylene base becomes a sled that also can carry other gear while being towed to the shooting site. Setting up and taking down the blind takes about 60 seconds. The spring-action roof opens automatically for an unobstructed shooting window. Two zippered side doors double as side windows. The rugged 500-denier Cordura nylon is both wind- and waterproof. The HayBale Blind is available in Advantage Wetlands camo, the official waterfowling camouflage of Ducks Unlimited. Available in two-shooter (28 pounds) and three-shooter (32 pounds) sizes.

Another blind I tested is the Ameristep Fieldhouse. It is an extremely lightweight, low-profile blind and can be backpacked into the field. The blind has an adjustable, low-profile field chair that converts into a backpack carrying system for the 8-pound, 24- by 2-inch blind case. A decoy bag shelf attachment strap allows you to carry any size of decoy bag on the blind shelf. The spring-steel construction provides easy setup and compact transport. One of the main features is the ripcord release springs that instantly pop the blind open when pulled and provide virtually 360-degree shots. The chair has an adjustable height so you can be in a liedown or sit-up position.

Underbrush has several waterfowl blinds, including their Classic (two-man) and Ultimate (four-man) blinds. Both models are made with dog door openings and have 3-D camo top openings. The blinds come fully assembled—no loose parts. Setup takes just seconds. Grasp the frame and with a flick of the wrist, pull it open, then step into the blind. The Ultimate has easy-to-open, "pop-thru" viewing and shooting windows with hook-and-loop clo-

The HayBale Blind from GooseView Industries looks exactly like a round hay bale. It features a heavy-duty folding aluminum frame, and the integral base serves as a sled for pulling decoys. (Photo courtesy GooseView)

The Ameristep Fieldhouse is an extremely low-profile blind for field shooting.

sures in the top. The blind includes anchoring stakes for windy days. For goose hunting the Goosebuster is a one-hunter, low-profile, portable hunting blind with a super-quick, bump-open top. It weighs just 5 pounds. The Hide Away Hunting blind is an all-purpose blind perfect for waterfowl. It's a basic three-panel blind with pre-attached spreader rods that weighs 2¼ pounds and accommodates one hunter.

Chrono Manufacturing Ltd. carries a variety of waterfowling blinds, mostly designed for goose hunters. Their Stealth Layout Field Blind is a low-profile model that will fit in a sport utility vehicle. It features all-welded steel tube construction, powder-coated paint, and a suspend seat system for comfort and to propel the hunter forward into a shooting position. The most interesting of the Chrono blinds, however, are their decoy blinds. Their Adjustable Goose Chair Decoy Blind allows hunters to conceal themselves and hunt effectively from within their decoy spreads. A camo nylon seat is designed to propel the hunter forward from a comfortable sitting position to a natural, relaxed shooting position. The hunter is concealed beneath a 40-inch-long, 20-inch-wide, and 12-inch-high goose shell with slots for viewing

The Chrono Manufacturing Goose Chair Decoy Blind appears to be a giant goose, yet provides concealment for one. (Photo courtesy Chrono)

incoming birds along the feather details. The unit sets up in 15 seconds and weighs just 10 pounds.

Quick Pro Blind is a spacious 6- by 5-foot blind that can be used in the field as a ground blind, as a pit blind cover, set up as a boat blind, or set in the marsh. The Quick Pro is portable, yet durable, and can be left up all season or backpacked for daily hunts. Options include Flip-Top (for complete overhead concealment and split-second opening), Extension Kit (expands the Quick Pro to a full 9 feet), Rainhood, Weather Curtain, and die-cut camo choices in reversible olive-brown and Shadow Grass Brown.

Outlaw Decoys has a wide variety of waterfowl blinds. Their Terminator Pro Guide is a low-profile model that accommodates one hunter, features a waterproof floor, and even has room to hide a dog inside. Their lighter-weight Annihilator Pro-Guide, low-profile blind features durable aluminum tubing that allows the sides to be dropped over your body for complete concealment. You can enter the blind from either end without stepping over the sides. The Outlaw Hay Bale Blind provides room for up to three hunters, resembles a hay bale, and comes on a plastic sled that allows you to take gear and decoys into

The Rotating Hunting Lounger from Semmler Products rotates 360 degrees and reclines in three backrest positions. (Photo courtesy Semmler)

Quick Pro produces a blind that can be used as ground field blind, a pit blind cover, as a boat blind, or set in the marsh. (Photo courtesy Quick Pro)

remote areas. The Assassin Goose Chair features 360-degree rotation so you can shoot in any direction. The steel tubing can handle hunters over 350 pounds, and the chair pin keeps the Assassin in place for quick retrieves from the blind without the blind falling over.

The G & H Buck Stumper is a quite unusual and extremely versatile blind. It is made of high-impact plastic and resembles a huge weathered tree stump. It will easily conceal one hunter on a folding stool; I've used it on land and even in shallow-water stump beds with great success. It can be assembled in minutes, yet is easy to pack.

WATER BLINDS

The Duck Dock, by Windsor Industries, is a spacious 4- by 8-foot deck that's large enough to comfortably hold three hunters and one dog. Featuring an excellent camouflage system, the Duck Dock is simple to erect. The unique interlocking design makes it possible for one person to perform the setup or removal in just 30 minutes. The Duck Dock is built of aluminum

A number of manufactured water blinds are also available, including the Cabela's Floating Coffin Blind, which provides a low profile for total concealment. (Photo courtesy Cabela's)

The Duck Dock features a 4- by 8-foot deck, enough room to hold three hunters and a dog. (Photo courtesy Duck Dock)

Trax America Duck Buggy is a quality two-man floating blind. (Photo courtesy Trax America)

with stainless-steel fasteners and comes with several choices of decking material. With its extremely stable platform, you get better shots than from a bouncing boat. And the sides and top provide protection from the wind and rain. The Duck Dock is designed for use in water up to 4 feet deep.

The Duck Buggy from Trax America is a quality two-man floating blind that features Advantage Wetlands camo and has a Quickshot flip top that allows shooting from a seated or standing position. The Duck Buggy has a hinged door for easy entry, a rain roof, and D-rings for conveniently towing or anchoring. Weight is 354 pounds and blind size is 4 by 6 feet. Load capacity is 1,000 pounds.

BLIND MATERIALS

If you wish to construct your own blinds or add further camo materials to a blind, a number of camo materials and accessories are available. FastGrass from Camo Outfitters, Inc., comes in mat form and quickly covers land or water blinds. Avery Outdoors offers their Real Grass blind material, mats woven from grass from deep in the jungles of Central America. Avery also

You can also create your own blind and easily camouflage it with any number of camouflage cloth, woven reeds and rushes, paints, and other materials available.

carries a full line of camouflage cloth, including their Die-cut Cerex and burlap. Hunter's Specialties carries a full line of camo-pattern nylon netting, burlap, and paints as well. If you need help in holding it all together, Manco has Camouflage Duck Tape. Underbrush carries a 3-D Tape that can add a finishing touch to the edge of almost anything. The tape is a varied width of leafy material that is up to 3 inches wide.

WARM FEET

Waterfowling often means hunting in bitter cold. Even in a blind and with the best of clothes and boots, you'll eventually get cold. Waterfowlers have used any number of ways to stay warm, including buckets of charcoal and catalytic heaters. Both the charcoal and older catalytic heaters, however, can produce poisonous carbon monoxide. The Coleman PowerCat catalytic propane-powered heater is suitable for indoors, which makes it ideal for use inside duck and boat blinds. The PowerCat heater employs platinum catalytic technology, which provides a flameless, whisper-quiet heat. Compact, lightweight, and portable, the PowerCat heater features push-button electronic ignition starting and operates for up to seven hours on a standard, 16.4-ounce disposable propane cylinder. In addition, the heater features a built-in fan, which operates on two D-cell batteries, to blow warm air out of the heater and to circulate the air. The heater can also be used without the fan switched on. The unit

Waterfowlers have been trying to keep warm in blinds for years. The Coleman PowerCat heaters can provide blind heat without the dangers of carbon monoxide.

puts out 3,000 BTU of heat. A sturdy, stable housing hides the fuel cylinder and fan blower while focusing the heater head in an upward-angled position.

LIGHT WHERE YOU NEED IT

One of the most difficult parts of waterfowling is being able to see in the black hours of early morning when putting out decoys and other chores. I've held a flashlight in my mouth many a morning while untying decoy bag knots. Three lights from Browning make the chore much easier. The Thunder Bug and Lightning Bolt compact lights clip to your cap bill. A flexible head directs a tightly focused 6,000-candlepower beam on the Lightning Bolt and 8,000-candlepower wide beam on the Thunder Bug. Both come in nonglare black with two AA batteries and night vision lens. For those wearing stocking caps in the bitter cold, the Cyclops headlamp has a comfortable headband and adjusts vertically. The Cyclops is available in 6,000- or 10,000-candlepower sizes in black with four AA batteries and two bulbs.

TOTING STUFF

Waterfowl blinds are quite often muddy and messy, and normally you also have a lot of stuff to tote to the blind. This includes shells, calls, flashlights, gloves, extra caps, lunch, and maybe a thermos of warm liquid. I've discovered three great totes. The Avery Floating Blind Bag features seven pockets for storage of all your equipment when in the goose or duck blind. And it will float up to four boxes of 3-inch magnum shells. It also has an adjustable shoulder strap with Avery's exclusive no-slip shoulder pad.

Both Browning and Flambeau offer hard blind boxes that can protect all your gear and keep it organized. The Flambeau model is 27 inches long with a handy lift-out tray. The Browning model also can be attached to a boat gunwale with unique clamps. And it has a watertight seal.

PRO TIPS

"Portable blinds are extremely important these days when hunting geese," said championship goose caller and expert goose hunter Fred Zink from Ohio. "Most goose hunting 10, 15, or 20 years ago was done in exact locations such as the Eastern Shore of Maryland, southern Illinois, Horicon Marsh, or other specific areas. Most of that hunting was done from pits or stationary blinds. But the local goose populations have exploded. I remember

If you prefer a hard-case tote, they're available from both Browning and Flambeau. The Flambeau model is shown.

15 years ago, and there were barely any Canada geese in Ohio other than at refuges. Now there are almost 200,000 resident geese. Geese have spread all across the countryside, not only Ohio and the Midwest, but from the East Coast to the West Coast; they all have huge populations of geese. This huge population is made up of small pods of geese on every farm pond, retention pond, river, golf course, everywhere. There are no longer exact locations where permanent blinds are effective for this type of goose and this type of hunting. You have to be mobile; you have to be able to hunt a particular field maybe once, then be able to move around. And when you move around, you have to have a concealment system that works and is very, very portable. The Avery Finisher Blind that we designed is a low-profile blind that folds up and is very easy to carry and transport. You can transport it in a small SUV; you can transport up to eight of them on a four-wheeler. It's very, very easy to transport. Portability is great, and it is adjustable to meet the hunter's size needs. It is low profile to hide away from the goose's view. The best kind of blind at all is the one that they can't see. The Finisher Blind is designed for 90 percent of the goose hunters in the U.S., those who are hunting the resident local geese."

12

WATERFOWL BOATS AND BOAT BLINDS

R egardless of whether hunting a marsh, river, small lake, or big open water, boats are a very important facet in many waterfowling situations. A waterfowl boat may range from a simple canoe to a johnboat, a boat designed just for waterfowling, or even a boat that can do double duty as a fishing boat as well. Following are some examples of the different types of waterfowl boats available.

WATERFOWL BOATS

CANOES

One of the most effective one-man boats I've used is the Poke Boat. At 22 pounds, it's light enough to easily car top but can be used to get into back-country marshes and explore small rivers. More of a kayak than a canoe, the Poke Boat can be tricky in rough water. The Coleman Scanoe is a fiberglass canoe with a squared-off stern that allows it to be powered by an electric

Boats are often a waterfowl necessity. They can be used to get back and forth to blinds, or even as blinds if camouflaged. (Photo courtesy The Duck Boat Company)

The Poke Boat weighs only 22 pounds, can easily be car topped, and is great for poking into protected backwaters.

trolling or tiny gas motor. The Fiber Pro sport boat is a canoe style with a square stern and is rated for up to 10 horsepower. The hull design makes the boat virtually untippable, and it's available in three camouflage patterns. Custom blinds are also available.

JOHNBOATS

Johnboats have been used as waterfowling boats from their very beginning. A small johnboat can be car topped or slid in the back of a pickup. Large johnboats, even as big as 20-footers, are great for building waterfowl blinds on and to carry several hunters. Remove the blind and you also have a good fishing boat. Triton, Lowe Roughneck, Alumacraft, Xpress, Waco, SeaArk, Tracker, and War Eagle offer a wide variety of johnboat sizes. An example is the 1650 DS from Triton, an all-welded aluminum boat that can do double duty as a fishing boat. It's 16 feet long with a 74-inch beam and is rated for five persons and 40-horsepower tiller steer. Many models are also available in camouflage and complete with dog ladders and gun boxes as well. Some of these boats feature tunnel hulls, which make them extremely shallow running.

The Coleman Scanoe is an excellent choice for transporting hunters in protected areas. (Photo courtesy Coleman)

Because of their versatility, johnboats are extremely popular duck boats and range in size from tiny car toppers to huge models that will carry numerous hunters and all their gear. Many, such as the SeaArk shown, come camouflaged these days. (Photo courtesy SeaArk)

SNEAK-BOX-STYLE BOATS

Boats are also designed just for waterfowling and include small sneak-box-style boats for shallow-water flats, marshes, and protected waters as well as small rivers. I've tested the Otter Stealth 1200 and it is perfect for protected waters. Constructed of molded, medium-density polyethylene, the Stealth is extremely rugged. It is 12 feet in length, with a weight of 85 pounds, and is available in marsh brown or olive drab. Seats, gun rack, shell holder, stabilizing pole holes, and handles front and back are molded in place. Dry storage compartments are located in both front and back. Several other manufactures offer these molded-plastic or fiberglass boats, including Outlaw, Carsten's, Bluebill, and Fiber Pro. Fiberdome creates handmade fiberglass boats the old-fashioned way, including their 12-foot Mallard, 14-foot Pintail, 14-foot 3-inch Widgeon, and 13-foot 6½-inch Redhead. All are double-ended, classic waterfowl skiffs. Carsten's Duck Boats, including their 10-foot Puddler, 13-foot 4-inch Pintail, and 14-foot 4-inch Canvasback, are available from Cabela's.

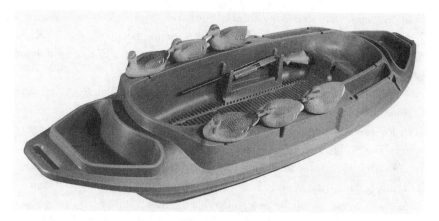

Sneak-box-style duck boats, such as the Otter Stealth, are low-profile boats used primarily in relatively protected waters. (Photo courtesy Otter Outdoors)

Created in the swamps and marshes of southern Louisiana, Cajun pirogues are great for negotiating shallow, narrow waterways. From Outlaw comes their Ghost waterfowl blind and boat, which can be used on dry land or water. The Ghost rolls on wheels or pulls like a sled on dry land or floats on shallow water or in flooded fields. It can also be paddled and accommodates one hunter.

The Outlaw Ducker classic marsh or small-water boat has a wide hull to provide great stability. The 12-inch profile, olive-drab finish, and built-in grassing cords make it easy to conceal. Rated for up to 2 horsepower or a 36-pound thrust electric trolling motor, the Ducker is also easy to pole. Closed-cell flotation in the deck and hull provides safety and quietness. The deck also features wave-breaking rails to keep hunter and equipment dry in rough water. An insulated floor and built-in backrest make the Ducker extremely comfortable. Space for shotgun shells, calls, and equipment is available in six vertical side and four deck pockets. The Ducker will fit into the back of a pickup.

The Duck Wrangler 14 has a removable blind that allows for three different shooting positions. The top can be flipped down for overhead shots, the side flipped down for out-front shots, or you can stand up and shoot with the top down as well.

The Duck Boat Company carries a full line of boats and boat blinds. Their TDB21 will accommodate five hunters, dogs, and gear. The molded hull and deck come standard, but you can customize the interior to suit. The boats are made of high-density cores or composite components with a stringer system infused over foam. Length is 21 feet 4 inches, beam of 7 feet 4 inches, and the boat is rated for 90/115 horsepower. Fourteen- and 17-foot models are also available.

The Arthur Armstrong line of duck boats from The Duck Boat Company includes the Sneaker, a 12-foot 6-inch one-man boat with 200-pound capacity. It's a low-profile nylon/fiberglass boat made for hunting marshes and protected waters. The Widgeon is 12 feet 4 inches but with a wider beam, and its cockpit offers room for two hunters and a dog. The Blackjack model is 13 feet 2 inches and will carry two men, a dog, and 350 pounds of gear. The Blackjack is rated for a 25-horsepower motor and includes a collapsible blindspray, matching motor cover, locking cockpit cover, two pedestal seats and bases, and a customized trailer.

The Osage Multi-Purpose Hunting & Duck Canoe is not really a canoe, but a 14-foot aluminum boat with a capacity of four persons and gear and a horsepower rating of 5. The low-profile boat is extremely stable and will float in 3 inches of water with two men and their gear. It has an optional removable blind with 360-degree visibility through viewing ports and two doors that operate independently. A fold-out ramp allows for safe nonslip entry for dogs. Remove the blind and it's an excellent shallow-water fishing boat.

SPECIALTY BOATS

The Coleman Crawdad is a molded, hunter-green boat that is easily car topped, and can also double as a great little fishing boat for protected waters. WaterQuest boats are molded of high-impact polyethylene hulls and are extremely rugged. The hulls absorb sound rather than amplifying it. They are also totally camouflaged with Realtree/Advantage camouflage using an exclusive patented process that laminates a no-peel, no-fade camouflage to the watercraft. The models include a 14-foot canoe, 15-foot 4-inch square-stern canoe, 10-foot 2-inch hunting/fishing boat, and 9-foot 4-inch utility boat along with an 11-foot 6-inch kayak. The boats are much less expensive than those manufactured of fiberglass, Kevlar, or Royalex. Camouflaged boat blinds, canoe and kayak spray covers are also available.

Outlaw Marine, of Outlaw Decoy fame, has several excellent waterfowling boats. Their top-of-the-line models are available in both 14- and

18-foot sizes. The 18-foot boat is designed for up to five hunters. Constructed of fiberglass, they feature a 7-inch-thick hull filled with sufficient closed-cell flotation to provide 320 percent of Coast Guard requirements. The boats have a V-bow design that has superior wave-breaking capability, and a keel provides for better turns. Trim tabs on the back help provide a smooth ride even at high speeds across rough water. The boats come with a fiberglass blind, which provides a total enclosure over the entire boat to protect hunters from wind, rain, and waves. The blind has grassing cords to help camouflage with natural materials and is easily removed at the end of the season, transforming the boat into a sturdy fishing boat. The blind features a rotating rain roof that is also adjustable in height or can be taken off completely. At its highest position hunters can shoot out of all four sides. Dropped down to the lower position, you can instantly rotate the roof and shoot up or to the sides. The roof can also be lowered completely and locked in place to protect your gear. A bow door, stern door, and gull-wing side doors all provide easy access to the boat. A walkway and safety harness anchors on the bow make it safe and easy to set out and retrieve decoys.

INFLATABLE BOATS

Several excellent inflatable duck boats are available. The Sevylor Layout Boat features a highly abrasion-resistant composite PVC and polyester hull; it is extremely tough, stable, and lightweight; and of course you can easily store it folded up in your closet or garage. Two shotgun slings, cargo platform for decoys or dog, D-rings around the cockpit to attach camo materials are standard features. An optional mount is available for an electric trolling motor.

Mad Dog Gear from Stearns has three inflatable kayaks all featuring Advantage Wetlands camouflage. They include one- and two-man models, and one also has a trolling motor mount. Tracking fins make them track like hard kayaks.

FOLDING BOAT

Then there's the folding Porta Bote, available in 8-, 10-, and 12-foot models in duck hunter olive green and with a square back for small motors. The boats weigh in at 49, 59, and 69 pounds respectively and fold up for storage.

The Porta Bote is a folding model that can easily be car topped and provides a stable duck hunting boat.

BOAT BLINDS

In addition to the boats that feature their own custom blinds, boat blinds are also available to fit almost any size of johnboat as well. The Avery Quick-Set Blind is one of the easiest to use and most effective boat blinds I've used. Once the Quick-Set is fastened to the boat, it can be erected or dropped down in seconds. In the up position, the Quick-Set Blind provides great camouflaging. In the down position, there's great visibility, and the camouflage doesn't get beat up when transporting or while boating to and from blind locations.

Innovative Wildlife Specialties PopUp Boat Blind has a full-coverage camouflage blind. It provides a warm, weatherproof interior with camo-net windows with roll-down storm flaps. A release lever triggers the top to open instantly for unobstructed 360-degree shooting. It attaches to boats with four C-clamps.

The Shelter Pro Underbrush Boat Blind has easy-open, shoot-through viewing and shooting windows with hook-and-loop closures. Fully assembled, setup takes just minutes with lightweight but industrial-strength aluminum tubing. Just grasp the frame and with a flick of the wrist pull it open and step into the blind.

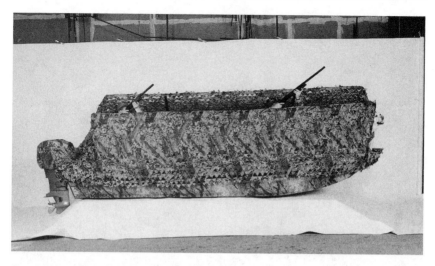

Custom blinds are also available for a variety of boats. The Avery Quick-Set Blind is the easiest and quickest to use. Once mounted, it can be set up for hunting or dropped down for travel in seconds. (Photo courtesy Avery)

Trax America also offers an easy-up and easy-down boat blind with a top that can be positioned for different shooting situations. (Photo courtesy Trax America)

The Cabela's Waterfowl Pontoon Boat combines the comfort and safety of a pontoon boat with the productiveness of a floating blind. An optional blind kit and trailer are also available. (Photo courtesy Cabela's)

Regardless of your waterfowl hunting waters, there's a waterfowl boat or boat blind to suit your situation.

13

WATERFOWL GUNS AND LOADS

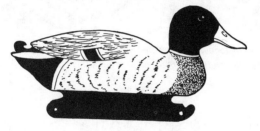

I began waterfowling with a 1907 Ithaca double side-by-side. It was choked modified and full, and was deadly on decoying ducks, as well as the Canada geese we occasionally hunted. When lead shot was banned, of course, I had to give up my favorite waterfowl gun. But the barrel was just about worn thin by then anyway. Most of us went to automatics or pumps with the advent of steel, and I tested some of the first "waterfowl" special guns, including a Browning and the venerable Remington 1100 SP. Then came the "drought" in waterfowling, and most gun manufacturers spent their time and energies on turkey guns.

With an increase in waterfowl numbers, gun manufacturers are again in the waterfowl gun business. The main difference these days is that most waterfowl guns are covered with camouflage. A number of traditional favorites are still around, but have been upgraded and camouflaged. Remington has the most to offer, including the 11–87 Super Mag Camo, their top autoloader, available in Mossy Oak Break-Up camouflage. The 11–87 Super Mag Camo comes with a 3½-inch chamber, Rem Choke, and has a 28-inch ventilated rib barrel.

Waterfowling guns and loads have become specialized over the years. Most guns used these days, such as the Beretta Xtreme, feature camouflage patterns and chokes matched to the situation.

The Remington 870 SPS Super Mag Camo is the waterfowling version of one of the most popular pump-action guns. It is available in Mossy Oak Break-Up, is also chambered for 3½-inch shells, and has a 28-inch barrel.

Remington also offers an SP-10 Gauge Mag Camo. This gun weighs 10.75 pounds and has a gas-operated cylinder, Rem Choke, and 26-inch ventilated rib.

Browning introduced the Gold Autoloader, which is available in both 10- and 12-gauge and with 3½-inch chamber. The waterfowl model comes with a backbored barrel with Invector-plus choke and Mossy Oak camouflage. The Gold Autoloader is available in 26-, 28-, and 30-inch barrels and also has a chamber lock.

Automatics, such as the Remington 1100, are the most popular types of waterfowling guns used these days. (Photo courtesy Remington)

Guns capable of handling 3½-inch shells, such as the Browning Gold, are great for goose hunting and some duck situations. (Photo courtesy Browning)

The Browning BPS is a pump available in Mossy Oak camo or black synthetic and has barrel options of 24, 26, 28, and 30 inches. The BPS is available in 12-gauge with 3½-inch chamber and backbored barrel with Invector choke. A 10-gauge version is available with the Invector choke, but the barrel is not backbored.

Winchester comes in with the Super-X2 Greenhead, almost the same exact gun as the Browning Gold, except it does not have the chamber lock. It has the 3½-inch chamber and a unique Greenhead protective finish that is green. The Greenhead comes with 28-inch barrel, Invector choke, and is available in 12-gauge.

The Beretta Xtreme has a feature allowing you to shuck out the shell from the chamber, and quickly insert another. This is great when you're hunting ducks and geese suddenly appear.

The Winchester 1300 Universal Hunter pump is available in 12-gauge, with Mossy Oak Break-Up camouflage. The 1300 has a 26-inch ventilated rib barrel with 3-inch chamber.

Beretta also offers several special waterfowl guns. The AL391 Urika gas-operated autoloader is a 12-gauge with 24-inch high-rib barrel featuring the exclusive MobilChoke System. It comes in Realtree camouflage and with a 3-inch chamber. Because of the popularity of the Urika, the A391 Xtrema was introduced. The Xtrema model will handle 3½-inch shells and is available in synthetic black, Realtree Hardwoods High Definition, Advantage Timber High Definition, and Advantage Wetlands. The barrel lengths include 24, 26, and 28 inches. The gun comes in a package including five OPTIMA-CHOKE Plus tubes and molded carrying case. It is the first shotgun to incorporate a rotating locking-bolt gas system, and has the ability to instantly change shotshells in the chamber.

Although KBI is well known for importing the Charles Daly doubles, they also carry the 3½-inch, 12-gauge MaxiMag autoloaders as well as pumps. The guns are available in chrome-lined and ported, 24-, 26-, and 28-inch barrels. The Field Hunter autoloader is available in Advantage Classic or synthetic black. The pump is available in black synthetic, Realtree Hardwoods, and Xtra Brown camouflage.

The Mossberg 835 Ultra-Mag pump gun is extremely popular with waterfowlers. It is chambered for 3½-inch shells and has a 28-inch overbored barrel with Accu-Mag choke system. The waterfowl model comes with Mossy Oak Shadow Grass or synthetic black stock.

The Spanish gun maker Benelli has two waterfowl autoloaders and a pump. The Super Black Eagle is an inertia-recoil-operated autoloader with a 3½-inch chamber. A twin to the Beretta ES-100, it's available in barrel lengths of 24, 26, and 28 inches, and with a special waterfowl camouflage of Realtree Xtra Brown. The gun is also available in black synthetic. The M-1 Field autoloader comes with a 3-inch chamber and features a Realtree Xtra Brown covering and five-choke system. The M-1 is also available in black synthetic.

The Benelli Nova pump is a 3½-inch chambered gun with Realtree Xtra Brown camouflage and a choice of 24-, 26-, or 28-inch barrels. Three chokes come as standard, and the gun features an optional recoil-reduction system. Set up for decoying waterfowl, the gun has only a 1¾-inch drop at the stock, which also creates a softer recoil.

The Franchi/Stoeger line includes two imported European brands of waterfowl guns. The Franchi 912 Variomax is a 12-gauge with 3½-inch chamber. The 912 includes a unique mercury weight recoil-reduction system that is built into the stock. It also features a dual safety and is available in 24-, 26-, 28-, and 30-inch barrels.

From Stoeger comes the Vursan Model 1200 autoloader, available in 12-gauge. It has 3-inch chamber, 26- or 28-inch chrome-lined barrels, and also features an inertia recoil system.

I had an old 12-gauge Marlin goose gun for many years, and although it was pretty good at goose hunting, it was best at local turkey shoots. It won turkey shoots to the point of almost being banned. The old gun is no longer being made, but with the purchase of H & R–New England Firearms, there's still a 12-gauge single-shot goose gun on the market. It comes with a 28-inch barrel and plain-Jane walnut stock. A 10-gauge single shot is also available with a 32-inch barrel with modified choke.

Ithaca Gun Works has the Model 37 bottom-ejection pump gun in Advantage Wetlands. A favorite for more than 60 years, the M 37 waterfowler is available in 3-inch chamber, 12-gauge with a special bored barrel, and Briley extended steel shot choke tube.

The Weatherby SAS (semi-automatic shotgun) 12-gauge shotgun comes in synthetic black or Mossy Oak Shadow Grass or Break-Up camouflage and is chambered to take 2¾- and 3-inch shells. It has a magazine cutoff for quick and easy loading and changing shells in the field. The self-compensating gas system provides for increased load versatility. The gun also features a special shim spacer system that allows you to fit the stock to different body shapes and sizes. An internal dampening system reduces felt recoil.

Ruger offers their popular Red Label over/under in an all-weather version that features a black synthetic stock and a corrosion-resistant backbored chrome molybdenum barrels. The barrels are 26, 28, and 30 inches. Four long, stainless-steel chokes come with the gun.

The Remington Model 332 over/under is a rebirth of one of the great field shooting classics—the Remington Model 32, a longtime waterfowling favorite. The Model 332 is available in a variety of 12-gauge vent-rib Rem Choke barrel options, from 26 to 30 inches. The Model 332 is a great waterfowling gun for those with an over/under tradition.

Other popular waterfowl guns include pumps and even doubles, such as the Remington 332 over/under. (Photo courtesy Remington)

SHOT

Shotshell loads have progressed as much as guns since I first started waterfowl gunning. Although a number of exotic nontoxic metal loads are available, most are fairly expensive, and many gunners still shoot steel. Winchester offers four steel shotshells for waterfowlers: Super-X Drylok High Velocity Steel, available in 12-gauge, 3 and 3½ inch, is a super-hot steel shotshell with 1,550 feet per second muzzle velocity; Super-X Drylok Super Steel with the exclusive Winchester two-piece double-seal wad for complete water resistance and a barrel-protecting shot cup to deliver a heavier load of steel shot in denser, more powerful patterns; Supreme High Velocity Steel featuring a specially formulated propellant that delivers steel shot at 175 fps faster than standard dry loads, plus the two-piece Drylok Super Steel wad and plated steel shot

Most modern guns feature interchangeable chokes, and a number of after-market specialty waterfowl chokes, such as the Marsh Max from Lohman, are available that can improve patterns. (Photo courtesy Lohman)

for denser patterns; Winchester Xpert Waterfowl steel shotshells combine a proprietary corrosion-resistant steel shot manufacturing process with superior Winchester components to produce a high-performance, value-priced steel shotshell.

Federal Premium Tungsten Iron offers nonsteel capabilities and is available in 12-gauge, 3 inch. Federal also offers their Classic High Velocity steel shot in 2¾- and 3-inch, 12-gauge loads at a reasonable price. The shells feature increased shot payload and high velocity, along with three watertight seals at the crimp, wad, and primer. The high-density cup prevents pellets from contacting the bore surface, while a high-output 209A Primer provides consistent ballistic performance at all temperatures.

Remington Nitro Steel High Velocity Magnum loads have a muzzle velocity of 1,500 fps, which allows for shorter leads and still produces dense patterns and high down-range energy. Offered in 12-gauge 3- and 3½-inch magnum loads, the steel shot is zinc-galvanized for superior rust resistance. These are a good choice for pass shooting or midrange decoying.

With the banning of lead shot for waterfowl, steel has been, and still is, the most common shot. It does not shoot the same as lead, and it's important to match the shot size to the waterfowl species and the shooting conditions.

WINCHESTER® DRYLOK™
State-of-the-art Steel Shotshell

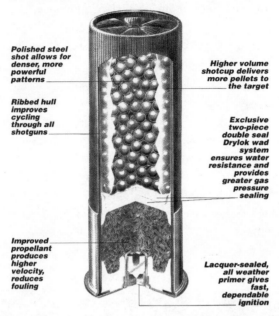

Polished steel shot allows for denser, more powerful patterns

Ribbed hull improves cycling through all shotguns

Higher volume shotcup delivers more pellets to the target

Exclusive two-piece double seal Drylok wad system ensures water resistance and provides greater gas pressure sealing

Improved propellant produces higher velocity, reduces fouling

Lacquer-sealed, all weather primer gives fast, dependable ignition

Winchester has come to the aid of waterfowl hunters with water-resistant shotshells. The Drylok system protects the new, cleaner, burning powder, which produces higher velocity and reduces fouling. Polished steel shot provides denser more powerful patterns, and the expanded shotcup helps deliver more pellets to the target.

Winchester continues to offer their Super-X Drylok Super Steel and Drylok High Velocity Super Steel shotshells, the official ammunition of Ducks Unlimited. (Illustration courtesy Winchester)

Remington Nitro-Steel and Express-Steel loads are extremely versatile, for everything from teal to the big honkers. The Nitro-Steel Magnum loads have greater hull capacities for the heavier charges and larger pellets necessary on larger waterfowl. They are excellent for pass shooting and midrange decoying. The Express-Steel loads are offered in 12-, 16-, and 20-gauge and include payloads suitable for everything from puddle ducks to divers. Both loads feature the Remington exclusive Rustless zinc-galvanized steel shot to prevent pellet corrosion and clumping in the hull, while primers and crimps are lacquered for increased water resistance. The Remington Sportsman Steel loads

Federal has both their Classic High
Velocity Steel Shot as well as their
Premium Tungsten-Iron shotshells
for waterfowling. (Photo courtesy
Federal)

are an economical high-quality load excellent for short-range, high-volume shooting during early duck season.

Remington's Hevi-Shot, manufactured in conjunction with Environ-Metal, Inc., is a proprietary alloy of tungsten-nickel-iron that has been approved throughout the United States for waterfowl hunting. The material has a 10 percent higher density than lead, which yields denser patterns and higher energy

The newer shot alternatives, such as Hevi-Shot from Remington, offer much the same shooting characteristics as lead. (Photo courtesy Remington)

than lead. The Premier Nitro Magnum Hevi-Shot loads are available in 10-gauge, 3¼-inch, and 12-gauge, 3- and 3½-inch lengths.

Bismuth Eco Ammo, which has a fiber wad and paper case, is available in 2¾-, 3-, and 3½-inch lengths and 12-, 10-, and even .410- and 28-gauge. Bulk Bismuth is also available for handloading.

CHOOSING

The choice of guns and loads for waterfowling is highly personal, and these days there's a wide diversity to choose from. If you prefer the traditional, an over/under or side-by-side loaded with nontoxic shot such as Hevi-Shot, can be extremely productive for decoying waterfowl, including both ducks and geese.

The most common choice is a semi-automatic or pump-action shotgun shooting one of the steel loads. Nontoxic shot, of course, will work in these situations as well.

Regardless of the gun you choose, it's extremely important to test pattern it with a variety of loads to determine the loads that work best with your spe-

Test pattern shooting is extremely important when choosing the best loads for your gun. Shoot at different yards with a variety of loads and chokes.

Protecting valuable guns while traveling to and from the blind is easy with the Avery floating gun case.

cific model. Do this with the gun locked in a gun vise or other type of bench-rest situation so you have consistent patterns. Shoot at a variety of distances, such as 25, 30, 35, 40, and 45 yards, to determine the different patterns. Use butcher paper with a 30-inch circle drawn on it to count pellets and determine the patterns.

14

SEASONAL STRATEGIES

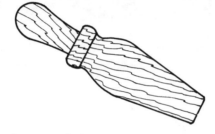

Waterfowl season begins with the early teal and, in some states, wood duck seasons, usually in September; then the major duck seasons begin in November and run into December or later, depending on the state. Goose season begins in early winter and runs until late spring, if you count the late snow goose season. In addition to the main seasons, special hunts or seasons for specific areas or the overpopulation of geese are also mixed in. As the season changes from early to late, the hunting conditions change, and the waterfowl's reaction to these conditions also change. It's extremely important to match the tactics to the season.

EARLY TEAL

Teal are the smartest dumb ducks. A flock of a dozen will strafe your blind in twisting, darting, fighter-jet fashion, often making a tantalizing second pass, yet offering almost impossible shots. The next time a handful of teal

The waterfowl season ranges from early fall through late winter and even into spring with the late snow goose seasons. Each season requires different decoys, gear, and strategies.

will placidly plop into your decoys before you know it, then you practically have to throw rocks at them to get them to flush.

These early birds offer some of the first waterfowl gunning of the season in many states, with an early teal season usually held sometime in September. Teal hunting is an opportunistic situation. Just like dove hunting, teal hunting depends on many factors, but the most important are weather and water. Teal prefer extremely shallow, mudflat sloughs, marshes, reservoirs, ponds, and lakes. The timing of cold weather in the northern breeding areas, causing the start of the migration, is also important. Teal seasons are typically short, and the seasons often miss the migration. Some years there's a season but no birds due to a late migration. Other years the birds migrate through before the season. If the birds migrate but find no water, as happens in much of the country in many years, they don't linger long at any stop, but continue their migration south. If food and water are available, teal may stay around for months, providing some of the best shooting at the start of the regular waterfowl season. Teal are never a given—but they are a tradition with many gunners.

HUNTING TACTICS

The first step is to locate the birds. If hunting public waterfowling areas, phone calls to the areas will usually reveal the teal situation. State waterfowl biologists can also provide information on the migration and populations. If hunting public reservoirs, coastal areas, large lakes, or marshes, scouting the areas a day or two before the season is extremely important. Look for mudflats with extremely shallow water. Use binoculars to identify birds using specific areas. Be ready to change hunting locations daily. Changing water levels from fall rains can affect preferred areas of the little birds. Also, don't expect the big flocks of birds you see with other waterfowl. Although teal may be plentiful, they typically don't travel in big flocks. And, as their migration can be over a period of time, local populations may vary day to day.

SETUPS

Teal will readily decoy to other puddle duck decoys, but they tend to decoy more readily to teal decoys. And those tiny decoys are part of the tradition. It doesn't hurt to add a pair or two of mallards to the set. The larger-sized decoys provide more visual attraction at longer distances. A couple of dozen decoys are all you'll need. Since the water is extremely shallow, decoy strings should be shortened accordingly. Teal tend to bunch up more than other ducks on the water, so decoys can be closer. A more open spread, however, creates a

The early teal season begins in hot weather. Teal aficionados prefer to use teal decoys for the tiny ducks, although they will decoy to mallard sets.

Teal sets should be placed fairly close to the blind, but with the decoys spread out.

bigger visual impact from a distance. Teal, like all waterfowl, land into the wind, and the decoy set should take advantage of the wind with a J- or C-shape and a landing pocket in front of the gunners. As decoying teal tend to come in close, even circling closer than the later, more wary waterfowl, the set can be kept fairly close to the gunners. Some companies make teal decoys using mallard molds, merely adding teal paint. The teal decoys from G & H, however, are the proper size and extremely realistic.

Shoreline vegetation is still quite rank in the early season, so creating a blind isn't as difficult as later. And since it probably won't be used for more than a couple of weekends, an elaborate blind isn't necessary. Many teal hunters simply wear full camouflage and hunker in the weeds, cattails, or rushes for the early season. A piece of net camouflage material, a couple of stakes, and a folding stool can also be used to create an "instant" blind when you find an area teal are using.

CALLING

Mallard calls can be used to bring in teal, but calls should be fairly sparse, with no highballs or other loud, demanding calls. Soft quacks, sit-down calls, and feeding chuckles work best. Widgeon whistles and teal calls, such as those from Primos or Haydel's, can also be used to add more realistic sounds.

GUNNING

Gunning for teal can be extremely humbling for expert gunners, and utter frustration for less experienced shooters. Twisting, darting, turning, flying at speeds of 50 miles an hour or more through trees and brush makes them extremely challenging. Like doves, they instantly go into an evasive-action mode at the first shot. The flock darts, explodes in all directions, then often comes around to taunt gunners after all shells have been expended.

As with most scatter-gunning, flock shooting is a problem. It's especially so in shooting these tiny targets, which tend to react as a group. It's extremely important to visually select only one bird and stay with it, no matter how hard. Follow-through shooting is the best tactic. Pick out a bird, swing with it, follow through, and shoot. Once hit, however, teal are not hard to bring down. "Light, fast loads, such as our new Xpert in 2¾-inch No. 4s with 1-ounce shot, would be my choice," suggested Mike Jordan, technical adviser with Marketing Services of Winchester/Olin. "Or you can use the 1¼-ounce, 3-inch No. 4s, but I don't think they're necessary for teal. If you're wading, the Drylok 2¾-inch, 1-ounce load would be a great choice."

Jordan shoots modified chokes for all his steel shot, but said it's extremely tight and suggested, "Improved cylinder might provide better patterns for fast-zipping teal."

Teal hunting is also an excellent time to bring out Granddad's old gun. Load it up with nontoxic shot, such as Bismuth or Hevi-Shot in No. 7s, and enjoy the challenge and rewards of old-time gunning.

KNOW YOUR TEAL

Teal, especially blue-wing teal, are some of the earliest migrators, often leaving their northern nesting grounds in August. Other species may also be around during early teal season, especially wood ducks and in some instances widgeon and gadwalls as well as a few mallards. Although teal are quite small compared to most other waterfowl and fairly easy to identify, it's especially important in the early season to properly identify your targets.

Blue-wing teal fly in very small, compact flocks of a half to a dozen birds. Because they migrate so early, blue-wing teal are often seen in the "ellipse"

Early Season

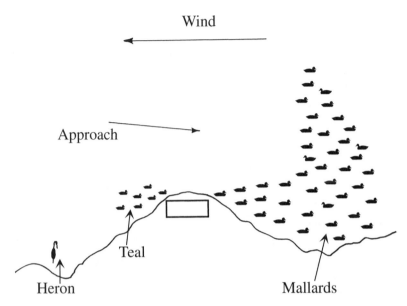

The first of the duck season also sees some teal in many areas, but most puddle duck gunners opt for mallard spreads. "We typically use about two dozen mallard decoys plus some teal," said Tom Matthews from Avery.

or molting phase, before they are fully feathered, making the drakes appear similar to the hens. The drake, however, has a dark belly while the hen's is lighter. The easily seen blue patch on the forewing is often the field mark; the iridescent speculum wing patches are dark green. Drakes utter a soft, whistling peep on the fly, while the hens occasionally utter a soft quack.

Green-wing teal are the smallest of the North American ducks. Their normal breeding range is farther north than the blue-wing, and although they begin migrating with the first cold weather, they linger along their migration route as long as open water is available. They also fly in erratic flights, twisting and circling as a unit much like barnyard pigeons, and are often found in larger flocks than the other teal. Drakes whistle and twitter, while the hens issue a soft quack. A whistling sound is made by the wings during flight. The male is a small, dark brown duck with a vertical white bar separating the spotted buff chest from the gray sides. A teardrop-shaped, green head stripe extending from in front of the eye coupled with a deep chestnut-colored head makes late-fall/winter identification easy. Early-season ellipse or juvenile drakes are harder to identify. The female is mottled brown and white. A green wing speculum is also found on green-wing teal, but with white banding on top and bottom. Green-wing teal are often called "partridge ducks" because of their explosive flushing nature.

Cinnamon teal are a familiar bird to gunners on the Pacific Flyway, although there is another population in South America. Found in smaller flocks than the other teal, cinnamon teal are very trusting birds and quite slow to alarm. The male is a dark red cinnamon, with light blue wing patches similar to those of the blue-wing teal. In flight the cinnamon teal is very similar to blue-wing, but in smaller groups. Cinnamon teal produce soft, nasal quacks and a low, growling chatter.

Blue-wing teal rarely tip up to feed. They collect floating bits of vegetation or food in water just a few inches deep. They require extensive mudflats with just inches of water. Green-wing teal tip up, as do cinnamon teal.

Teal hunting is often a hot, mosquito-ridden affair, but a brace of the little birds provides some of the most challenging gunning and the makings of an exquisite dinner.

EARLY- TO MIDSEASON DUCKS

"We hunt the early- and midseason mallards in the green timber around Stuttgart, Arkansas," explained Tom Matthews, president of Avery Outdoors, manufacturers of quality waterfowling gear. Tom and his buddies regularly hunt the famous Bayou Meto near Stuttgart. "At that time we use just two dozen mallard decoys in the woods because you don't need a huge number when you're hunting flooded timber bottoms."

My son Mark, a waterfowl guide on Truman and Stockton lakes in Missouri, primarily hunts the middle zone of Missouri on Truman Reservoir, and the season typically opens in mid-November. As he describes, and I personally know his front porch illustrates, during the first week or two he'll hunt 200 to 300 decoys just to stay competitive. Mark mixes lots of big magnum decoys with the teal decoys, because typically during that time, the majority of ducks will be teal, with some local mallards and wood ducks—actually almost any-

Midseason

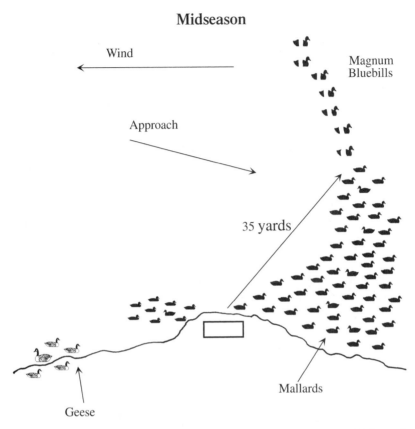

Mark Burch may hunt with as many as 300 decoys on the big reservoirs near his home during the early and midseasons. He mixes big magnum mallards with teal and bluebill sets.

As the season progresses and the birds become more wary, or stay around and become "local" ducks, Mark cuts back on both calling and decoy numbers.

thing on Truman. Mark hunts the backwaters and sloughs off the main river channel. As the season progresses, he scales down everything—fewer decoys as well as less calling.

LATE-SEASON DUCKS

Some will argue—but only because they haven't been there. Late-season ducks are the toughest game in town. Even if you don't die, and some duck hunters do, it can mean frostbitten fingers or, at the very least, some of the most uncomfortable times you'll experience. Late-season waterfowling also offers the best of the sport. At times, lots of birds. Challenging birds that have survived the migration from north to south. These are truly sky warriors. You'll earn every mallard curl or bright goldeneye you collect. At other times, it's ridiculously easy. Storm-driven birds pour into potholes and spring creeks, weary and looking for comfort.

"At the end of the season everything shallow freezes in Arkansas and we move down into Mississippi to the flooded cypress brakes off the Mississippi River," said Matthews. "Those river sloughs get deep in places, especially if you've had a wet year, and they rarely freeze. They're rest areas, not a food source at all like hunting the flooded timber. Ducks at that time are looking for as much confidence as they can get. They've been hammered on and shot at all season by the boys up north.

"You get bigger groups, and you need bigger decoys. We've also started throwing in about six big white pintail drake decoys because they show up a mile away and they look natural. We don't kill many pintails but we do see some in late January, and it's something that seems to add a lot of confidence to our spread. We also use a weighted-keel decoy because we're hunting deeper water and it's easier to toss them out and know they'll land upright."

Tom also feels you should keep your decoys absolutely clean, especially in the late season when ducks become more wary, and suggests scrubbing with soap and water, especially if they've been hauled around muddy fields or shallows and are coated with mud. He prefers G & H decoys because he feels they're not only the most realistic, but the paint job holds up to his vigorous cleaning chores. He also uses only Tanglefree decoy line with 6-ounce strap weights and about 20 feet of line per decoy so he can move and adjust to situations.

"We rig them with about 18 to 20 feet of line," said Tom, "Because the Mississippi River late in the season is often affected by floodwater, and we try to stay mobile. A lot of guys stay and try to make it happen but if it doesn't, we move. We'll pick up decoys and move 50 feet, or even 20 feet. I also wrap with the figure-8 on the back rather than around the keel because you can really do it fast, and we're often moving to a different place."

Missouri has a north zone, central zone, and southern zone. As we move into the southern zone, Mark Burch moves to Stockton Reservoir and again begins with big spreads, then downgrades as the ducks become more decoy- and call-wary.

"By the end of the season lot of folks are overblowing calls, using big spreads," Mark explained. "Birds coming out of the north are literally getting hit hard with decoys and calls. Then we go completely opposite, and may even get down to a dozen decoys in a backwater cove at the tail end of the season, and just a call or two.

"In the very last part of the season, on the main lake, we'll almost go to a full diver spread and a dozen mallards. Mallards will decoy readily to diver ducks, if they're set right, and we see a lot of diver ducks on the bigger reservoirs."

A few years ago Missouri was holding thousands of late-season ducks on the reservoirs, marshes, and waterfowl management areas. Overnight the temperature dropped from the 30s to 10 below. Ponds, potholes, marshes, and the

Late season offers some of both the easiest and toughest duck hunting.

shallows of the reservoirs froze solid. Mark discovered a tiny creek no more than a half dozen feet across, fed by a spring on the bank. The creek was in an open dairy pasture, and the tiny spring-fed pothole swarmed with hundreds of mallards when we arrived. During a driving sleet storm we flushed the birds, hunkered against the bank within a few yards of the pothole, covering ourselves and Mark's Chessie with a white sheet. The birds attempted to get back into the pothole while we were still setting up. Within a matter of minutes we had collected two limits of drakes and were watching a waterfowler's dream. Literally hundreds of birds funneled back into the pothole as we watched in awe. My fingers and toes were numb by the time we got back to our truck.

That's the key to ducks late in the season—bad weather and lots of it. The worst scenario is warm weather across the United States during duck season. Without bad weather, especially weather cold enough to freeze ponds and marshes, and if food is available, many ducks simply don't fly south. Knowledgeable late-season gunners constantly monitor the Weather Channel. When December and January storms collect in the Dakotas, sweeping across the northern tier of states, ducks move ahead of the storms.

The moving water of rivers and spring creeks offers the best opportunities, and quite often a hidden, out-of-the-way pocket can hold more ducks than you can imagine. Mobility is important. In most instances you'll need nothing more than a camouflage cloth, or even a white sheet, thrown over you and your dog and companions. Or the material can be draped over wooden stakes.

Closing-time ducks don't require many decoys. In fact, the fewer the better, as late-season ducks are quite often decoy-shy. A half dozen, or at most a dozen, of your best-quality decoys is the best choice. Motion, floating decoys can also help keep the water from freezing.

Late-season ducks are call-shy. It's hard to do, but sometimes the best tactic is to simply pocket your call. At most call sparingly and only with soft sit-down calls and individual quacks.

A proper decoy set is one of the major keys to success at this time. It's extremely important to match the decoy set to the hunting situation. Sometimes fewer decoys is the best choice, especially for decoy-shy birds. At other times the larger the spread, the better.

The standard decoy set patterns are effective. A J-, hook, C-, or V-pattern will be productive; the exact pattern is not as important as the location of the decoy set and paying close attention to the wind. Location, location, location are the three keys to decoying ducks. You simply have to be where the ducks want to be. Many successful late-season hunters look for small pockets, areas that are out of the way, even hard to get to. "We hike back farther than anyone else," said Matthews. The public hunting area receives a lot of pressure, but Tom has figured out a few tricks that produce when everyone else is coming up empty handed. "It's sometimes hard work, but you can't argue with the results."

If hunting local ducks or those that have hung around an area for a long time, especially on public lands, the best bet is to downscale your set. Although my son Mark and I often use close to 100 decoys at the beginning of the season, the last week or so finds us with a couple of dozen on open water and a half dozen on flooded timber and small potholes.

Traditional decoy lore is that the set should be spread out, with the decoys well separated. Tom Matthews has found the exact opposite to be the best bet for the late-season, decoy-shy ducks in the flooded timber he hunts. "We bunch a couple of dozen decoys in an area the size of a washtub, with only three or four separated," said Tom. "Sounds strange, but if you watch when ducks come into these areas they land in a tight wad, then swim apart. I think

Tom Matthews said you really have to stay mobile in the late season. He may move decoys just 50 feet to make the set more appealing.

the tight grouping in this case makes the ducks think other ducks have just landed, and they just barrel right on in."

We always add Canada goose decoys to our set, with just one or two at the first part of the season, then gradually adding more. By the end of the season we may have more geese than duck decoys, but the ducks decoy readily to the spread. Some gunners take only a half dozen Canada floaters to hunt ducks in the last few days of the season.

Many diver ducks are the last to migrate. If hunting open water, use either a full diver set or combine divers with puddle ducks. Don't, however, mix them together; make separate sets. Position the puddle ducks close to the blind or shore with the diver sets out in the open and as an attractor. The reason? Puddle ducks don't like to fly over other ducks, but divers will do so readily. Mark likes to place the diver ducks on a long string leading out into the lake. The Cabela's Decoy Gang Rig makes this easy to do.

Don't overlook field hunting for mallards and other puddle ducks in the latter part of the season. Feed fields that attract geese bring in these birds as well. In this case a large spread of field mallards combined with Canada geese—the two separated, with blinds in the middle—can be the most effective set.

Use only the best and most realistic decoys you have. Make sure all the season's accumulated mud and grime is cleaned off. If hunting in sleet or a snowstorm, make sure you keep the decoys cleaned off. The weight of the sleet or snow can make them sink sideways and have an unnatural appearance. Even if the birds are flying, the best bet is to go out and keep your decoys maintained rather than sitting in the blind and hoping the birds won't notice. Flagging can add to decoy effectiveness in the late season.

In many cases you'll be hunting skim ice in the late season. Break a hole in the ice and set decoys in the hole. Also set some field decoys out on the ice. Ducks and geese both regularly rest on ice. If hunting on water and it begins to freeze, make sure you maintain an opening around your decoys. The latter part of the season is the one time I use motion decoys. I've found that ducks especially become extremely wary of the wing-flapping motion decoys as the season progresses. Last year, to test this, we set and pulled motion decoys throughout an entire hunt. Guess what? When they were out the birds invariably spooked. The kind that work in the water, moving the decoys about, however, are extremely effective in the late season. These types of motion decoys can also be used to keep the water from freezing.

Late Season

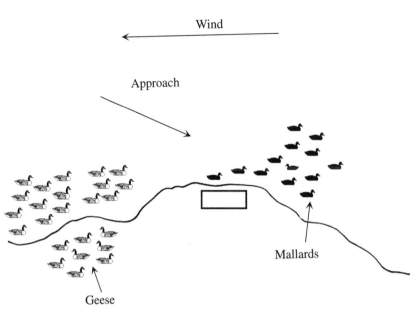

By the end of the season many birds have become call- and decoy-shy. Mark often cuts back to a handful of duck decoys and adds a couple dozen floater Canada goose decoys to the set.

I'll never forget one late-winter hunt. Tom Matthews and I simply sat in awe as we watched the spiral begin. At first a half dozen mallards dropped from the sky, down through the tops of the flooded green timber and onto the coffee-colored water in front of us. Then a couple more dozen, followed by dozens more, and then it began to virtually rain ducks. We had just collected our limits of drake mallards and were picking up decoys when the flight came in. We just sat and watched and grinned at each other. When mallards commit to a green-timber honeyhole, it's an experience serious waterfowlers don't forget. And when thousands come in, it's an experience of a lifetime. It's only happened to me twice in almost half a century of waterfowling. Both times occurred in the last few minutes of the season. And you don't have to be on an exclusive private club for it to happen. Tom, his friends, and I were hunting one of his favorite public-use areas in the heart of the Mississippi Delta.

I also remember another hunt my son Mark and I had on a Corps of Engineers lake near our home in the very last of the season. Like the Mississippi hunt, when ice covers everything but the hole you've chopped, you quite often have the hunting to yourself, except for the ducks. In fact, you will often see more ducks in a single day than the entire rest of the previous season. The major factor is timing—you have to be on the water when the ducks come through. On my Mississippi hunt I had left Missouri on the front of a severe winter storm—Mark and I had a great day just before I was to fly out. I almost didn't get to Mississippi due to the storm shutting down some airports. When I arrived that afternoon, Tom was ecstatic. "We didn't have but a handful of local ducks last week," he related. "But the marsh is absolutely full of them now. They just came in today!"

Unfortunately, friends in Arkansas never even saw the ducks them due to the severeness of the storm. The ducks overflew Arkansas to the south, and they didn't get any last-minute shooting. But that's last-minute waterfowling; you simply have to be on the water or ready to go at the drop of a hat—or rather, weather. The key is to watch the national weather news and hunt the days preceding a major storm that begins north and sweeps across and down the nation.

The first step is finding the ducks, and once things begin to freeze, waterfowl often change habitats. "Late in the season you need to look at the rivers and hot-water power plant lakes," said Fred Zink. "If you're hunting Canada geese, the migrating geese have usually moved through, leaving you with the locals, and they're really smart by that time. Late in the year, here in Ohio, most of the ponds, lakes, marshes, and reservoirs freeze up, and most people think the ducks leave, but they go to the rivers. Try to find a spring-fed river. They typically are smallest, but almost never freeze. They also usually have aquatic vegetation such as watercress, eelgrass, something the ducks can feed on. If there's snow on the ground here, the ducks will definitely be on rivers, because that's usually the only food source. Also, the big reservoirs are not too productive when snow covers the ground, because the puddle ducks can't go feed in the fields, and the reservoirs are typically too deep and have no vegetation for feed."

In Missouri, however, Mark and I find that the bigger reservoirs are great for late-season ducks—unless they freeze over. Then we also head for the rivers.

"We think less is better at the end of the season when it comes to decoys," said Tom Matthews. "Twenty-four decoys is about it."

"On geese, the smarter the birds, the less decoys." said Fred. "I would recommend using anywhere from two decoys to no more than a dozen and a half, and only the best full bodies."

"When hunting on public reservoirs you need to hold your ducks tight to your spread because you're not the only ones out there," said Mark. "Early in the season we use a lot of teal teasers, but in the late part of the season we change decoys and use diver rigs and goose rigs on the reservoirs. We also see lots of species variety, so you need to be extremely versatile. At that time color is a major contributor to decoy deployment."

Fred emphasized the need for Canada goose decoys in the spread for ducks. "Early-season mallards typically won't light with goose decoys, but as soon as the late-season migration shows up, they'll usually pitch to a Canada goose decoy set five to one over duck decoys. I would use as many Canada goose decoys as possible, even more goose decoys than mallard decoys."

Decoys with jerk strings, and water motion decoys are also good to add in late winter. These not only add to the realism of the set but can also be a help in keeping freshly chopped holes from freezing back over.

Diver ducks are often the last to migrate. Adding diver decoys to your spread can increase your chances for success.

All three experts agreed, the less calling the better. "We all like to hear ourselves call—it's half the fun," said Tom. "Late in the season when the ducks are getting wary, however, we actually make a decision on who is going to call and everybody else puts their calls up. When the ducks come in, you'll see everybody start grabbing for their calls. It's a hoot, but it works on the super, super-wary ducks."

Mark agreed calling should be minimal. "If birds are under a lot of pressure from other hunters in the area you need to 'coax' them in with a lot of soft single quacks and three- to five-note calls, a lot of feed calls. Leave the contest, show-off calling at home. Long, repetitious calls just don't work. Widgeon whistles are good to add in during late season."

"Call only when and if you have to," said Fred. "We've found the best tactic is not to call at all. If you're a very accomplished caller, calling doesn't hurt, it can help, but if you're an average hunter I would recommend not calling."

Concealment is a problem in late season because much of the natural vegetation is down. "Where I hunt, by the latter part of the season, the boat blind is out of play," said Mark. "It's hard to hide to begin with, and by late season the ducks steer clear of the big floating gunships. We use natural vegetation blinds or flooded timber. It's also extremely important to dress for the best concealment in the natural surroundings. For instance, marsh hunters would do well with Mossy Oak Shadow Grass, but when hunting the tree rows and points of big reservoirs, or especially flooded timber where you simply stand against a tree, the best choice is a darker, more muted hue, such as Mossy Oak Shadow Branch."

LATE-SEASON GEESE

To be successful with late-season geese you'll need lots of decoys. Some of the most challenging and exciting gunning is for Canadas over the water, but it takes large numbers of bulky decoys. The bad part, however, is that the decoys must be extremely realistic. I've found the Cabela's Exclusive Big Foot Canadas hard to beat.

Field shooting requires even more decoys, with several hundred not an unusual number. Again the set is usually with the blind or blinds located in the center of the set and with an open pocket downwind for the geese to land in.

The past few years has seen a major emphasis on late-season snow and blue goose hunting, with some seasons running into early spring. In this case

For late-season geese you'll need lots of decoys.

you'll need lots of decoys. Experienced gunners use some shell decoys, lots of silhouettes, and even the famous Texas Rag sets.

SAFETY

Late season can be dangerous. Follow all safe boating rules. Wear a PFD. Carry matches, fire starter, and a safety blanket, or a change of dry clothes, in a waterproof container. Tell someone where you will be going and when you expect to return. Be aware of frostbite problems. Wear neck and face protection as well as adequate gloves.

PRO TIPS

"During the early teal season we don't use mallard decoys; we actually use teal decoys," said Tom Matthews. "I think ducks know different ducks and we use about three dozen teal decoys, but primarily as confidence decoys because of the way teal buzz the set. Teal hardly ever come in and land the first time, but they will eventually come in and land. It takes those confidence decoys, just a few whistles and calls—and patience. We place the decoys so when the teal buzz in and eventually sit down they are going to sit down right in front, and when they leave it is going to give us good shots. Teal are tough to hit on the fly; what we're trying to do is minimize the difficulty of hitting them by placing the decoys so they have to fly right in front of us when they arrive and when they leave."

"During the early teal season we use small spreads," said Mark Burch. "Normally about three dozen G & H teal decoys, along with about a dozen mallards. We may even add in a pair or two of wood ducks. We hunt public land, shallows, backwater sloughs, mudflats, even some flooded timber—all the good little teal holes."

15

ADVANCED DUCK HUNTING STRATEGIES

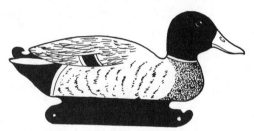

Although it's not quite pitch dark, dawn is still a bit away. We're in the decoys, untangling lines, tossing blocks into a semblance of a flock of ducks, whispering among ourselves, the excitement of opening day growing with each moment. A sudden flurry of wings and a half dozen green-wing teal try to sit down among us. We anxiously speed up our efforts; finally the last decoy is out and we scurry to the makeshift blind. We look at our watches again, and again, and again. Still minutes until shooting time and four more batches of teal have dropped into our decoys, nonchalantly swimming among their silent brethren. Then a half dozen widgeon drop in as well, and the waiting gets tougher.

"Mallards at 4:00," my son Mark whispers tensely. "What time is it?"

"Shooting time," declares Scrappy, glancing at his watch and the shooting time chart.

"Now what," whispers Harold, sitting next to Scrappy. "Do we take the ducks we have in hand, or try for the mallards?"

Mark doesn't answer; he's already on his call, giving coaxing sit-down calls to the dozen or so mallards that have disappeared behind our blind. We hear the quack of the lead hen, and a few soft quacks answer from our decoy set. Mark wisely shuts up, and the mallards make a swing in front of the blind, just past our last decoy and out of range, then disappear again behind the blind. It's so still the blind and its inhabitants, including Mark's Chessie, could be statues. Even though this is my fortieth duck season opener, I can feel my heart begin to pound in anticipation.

"Take 'em!" Mark exclaims and we jump to our feet. In front of us is absolute pandemonium. The flock of mallards seems to hang for a second right in front of the blind, big red feet and legs waving absurdly as they always do on their descent. Then the flock turns in an instant, wings beating desperately for altitude. The ducks in the decoys are also scrambling, the teal springing upward in a spray of water and the widgeon coming off the water like they were jet propelled. It's a mass of ducks flying in every direction, the noise of the shotgun barrage lost in the confusion.

Suddenly it's quiet, the smoke clears, and feathers and ducks drift on the rippling water. "Only six ducks from four hunters," Mark laments. "Boy, we're lousy! Guess it was kind of a confusing opener, but man that was fun!"

PUBLIC RESERVOIR AND LAKE STRATEGIES

The hunt described occurred on Truman Reservoir near my home. It's an example of the type of public waterfowling you can experience on any number of reservoirs scattered around the country, as well as on the bigger natural lakes and the Great Lakes. And it's relatively free, as opposed to paying high rates for leased land or to belong to a club.

LAND-BASED

You don't even need a big, high-priced boat to hunt the big waters. There's lots of great hunting from the shore if you do a little "footwork." Most Corps of Engineers reservoirs have ample public lands surrounding their lakes. Some provide great waterfowling, others don't, depending on the geography of the land. Flat uplands and flooded marshlands edging the lake provide the best opportunities. These areas normally are in the upper or headwaters areas of the lake.

Many lakes and reservoirs offer great public waterfowling, and in many cases you don't even need a boat, as shown here on Kerr Reservoir in Kansas.

Use a topographical map to locate these spots. Look for shallow coves and flats. Long main lake points that protrude far out into the lake can also be great spots, even in deeper water. These can provide excellent goldeneye and scaup hunting later in the season. Use a good lake topographical map, such as those from Fishing Hot Spots, to locate these spots.

And you'll probably have to do a bit of walking to get to the best spots. Most of these areas are closed to vehicular traffic. Mark has designed a light-weight, one-wheeled "travois" of aluminum tubing and bicycle tires that can carry his blind and large numbers of decoys to these out-of-the-way places. Many of these areas also don't allow permanent blinds, so a lightweight portable blind is essential.

BOATING

Most of the hunters on the big waters, however, utilize boats to get to hunting spots where they may have floating blinds or can erect portable blinds. "We hunt just offshore of Saginaw Bay on Lake Huron," said Mark Bussard, expert waterfowler. "At most this would be a couple of hundred yards right off the shoreline on the outside of the reed islands. It's simple hunting. We normally use a boat to haul our decoys, spread out our decoys, push the boat into the reeds, and simply sit on marsh seats. There's really a diversity of species on the big waters. You just never know what types of ducks or waterfowl will come in, so you need to be set up to attract all of them. It's always a good mixed bag of ducks. We shoot mallards, black ducks, and wood ducks, but they probably make up only around 20 percent of our seasonal take. We get a lot of redheads, an awful lot of bluebills, the canvasbacks are good, and we get widgeon, a few pintail, and an awful lot of buffleheads and geese. We get cackling or lesser Canada and a lot of greaters as well.

"Wind is always a major factor when hunting these shallow-water areas of the big lakes. The direction of the wind dictates how deep the water will be, and the location, including the specific reed island we hunt each day."

Boat blinds are becoming increasingly popular as well. These range from big boats with a totally enclosed blind, with gunners secure from all elements, to small, makeshift blinds constructed on boats used for fishing as well as for duck hunting. "Concealment is a definite main requirement in hunting anywhere, but especially on the big water, because it's harder to hide in that situation," said Mike Ward, president of War Eagle Boats. "It's extremely important to find a background that will blend in with your particular boat camouflage. We build boats from 12 to 23 feet long and we offer them in the various Mossy Oak camouflage patterns, just like the clothing, to allow our boats to blend in with a variety of waterfowling conditions. And we camouflage all the components of our boats, not just the sides and hull. This allows them to blend in a little bit better with their surroundings. We also offer Avery Quick-Set Waterfowl Blinds on our waterfowling boats to complete the package. They are simply great because you can set them up and down extremely quickly, and from a safety viewpoint we feel they're great because you can drop them down when you're running and see a lot better than boats with the permanent covered blinds over the top. This also makes it a lot easier to trailer the boat and blind on the highway."

TACTICS

In the early part of the season big-water ducks are quite often fairly "local"— or ducks that trade around the water from cove to cove. At first they're easy, but they quickly become call-, blind-, and decoy-shy. Son Mark insists that everyone in his blind wear full camouflage including gloves and face masks, just like turkey hunters, to prevent ducks flaring from upturned faces. And everyone must have a camouflaged gun, or camouflage to cover it. He meticulously grasses his blinds, continually changing or adding netting, grass, tree branches, and other cover-type items to keep his blind fresh and provide plenty of cover.

Calling varies from extremely aggressive to almost nothing, depending on the conditions. You can often see ducks trading a long way on open water and long, hard, highballing is sometimes the case to get their attention. Big-reservoir ducks can, however, get hit pretty hard, and it is easy to overcall. Mark Burch likes to give moderate, fairly soft welcome and feeding calls every 15 minutes or so for those ducks that are out of sight, but may be fairly close.

"Because of the variety of ducks, we have several different types of calls along," said Mark Bussard. "The area we hunt is a feeding area, so we blow the mallard feed call the most and use the hail call very sparingly. Here we hail

Because of the variety of waterfowl available on the big water of lakes and reservoirs, it's important to have a variety of decoys in your set.

call just until we see ducks turn, regardless of how far out they are, then switch to an occasional quack or lone hen. We also have whistle calls and diver calls for when the bluebills, cans, and other divers come in."

At the first of the season, figure on a big spread; 100 decoys isn't unusual for Mark Burch to set out. By midseason he cuts way back to a couple to three dozen decoys to attract decoy-shy ducks. Then in the latter part of the season, when and if—and it is often a big *if*—new flights of ducks are forced down through our area from the northern states, he goes back to big spreads to attract the newcomers.

"We typically set out four dozen mallards, using magnum or super mags," said Mark Bussard. "All the bodies are larger than standard. We set up a typical mallard hook close to the reed island we're hunting. We set a half dozen goose decoys off to one side and then place about four to six dozen diver decoys—typically bluebills—and run a straight-line spread, about 25 yards out off the mallard hook. We run about 8 feet of line off our decoys to get a good, natural-looking position as they sit on the water, and we definitely use a dog."

If you're looking to add some excitement to your season, try big-water waterfowling. You may find, like Mark Bussard, you'll limit out by 11:00 A.M.

SAFETY

Big water can mean danger. Two waterfowl hunters lost their lives on Truman a few years ago, and a father and his two young sons almost did. My son Mark went down in a boating accident on Stockton Lake in central Missouri several years ago, in 20-degree weather. Luckily a tree was nearby. Three duck hunters also survived a cold, stormy night on Toronto Reservoir in Kansas when a fast-approaching storm made crossing the lake to get back to their automobile impossible. In both latter cases the hunters followed one extremely important survival rule—they told someone where they were going and when they expected to return. When they didn't return, someone came looking.

Following are safety rules for big-water waterfowlers:

1. Make sure you inform someone of where you are going and when you expect to return.
2. Have certified personal flotation devices that fit everyone in the boat and make sure they're worn at all times when boating.

3. Do not overload the boat. This is a very common waterfowling mistake with hunters, lots of decoys, a dog, and other gear. Weigh your gear and check the total weight rating of the boat.

4. Follow safe boating rules and don't take chances. High wind and waves can develop quickly. You may be better off staying put on land or getting to the nearest land and staying rather than making rough-water lake crossings.

5. Take a boating safety course to learn how to boat in rough water.

6. Carry a survival kit in a waterproof pack. It should include: a first-aid kit, spare batteries for flashlights, spare flashlight, flares, a small propane stove, dehydrated food, space blankets, and hurricane matches. Spare clothing in a waterproof bag can also be invaluable to help prevent hypothermia in case of a swamping.

7. Understand the rule-of-three for signaling for help. Three shots, three sticks or oars stuck in the mud or sand, or three piles of rocks are all international signals of distress.

8. You may wish to consider carrying a marine radio—it's extremely good insurance and costs are going down. Those with weather bands can prove invaluable.

9. Carry a lake map, compass, and GPS, and understand how to use them.

10. Learn to recognize hypothermia and treat it.

WIND STRATEGIES

Wind is the single most important factor in waterfowling success. Too little and the action often dies down—too much and shooting becomes exciting, but also more challenging. Sometimes too challenging. Waterfowl land into the wind, and setting the decoys properly to position landing ducks or geese for the best possible shooting is the first step. When using portable blinds, or hunting without blinds, merely hiding in the shoreline vegetation, locating the proper blind or hunter position in relation to the wind, is fairly easy. In many instances, however, shoreline blinds are fixed. Blinds on managed waterfowl areas and many private duck or goose clubs are permanent affairs, often elaborately constructed. Locations for blinds on public-use areas such as reservoirs, large lakes, and marshes are also often limited due to land configuration. The task, then, is to position the decoy set to take advantage of the wind direction.

Most duck sets for open water or marshes, ponds, and lakes are in the shape of a J or tilted C, with the main body of decoys in the lower part of the J or C and a longer arm extending out into the water to create a landing pocket. The J or C can be turned in a variety of ways to suit the wind. Regardless of the angle of the set, the farthest decoy creating the pocket should be no more than 35 yards from the blind. In order to cut down on cripples while shooting steel shot, this should be about the distance limit of shots taken, even with ducks right over the pocket. If your blind is surrounded by water, place a handful of decoys behind the blind to act as confidence decoys. These are especially effective on wary birds that tend to circle several times before landing.

Always keep a weather eye on the wind direction. A piece of dark thread tied on a branch or to the blind provides a mini wind sock. If the wind changes, change the decoy spread. Even if you spook a few birds while moving the set, the results are usually worth it. Those hunting flooded timber will find wind not as much a problem where waterfowl are more confined in their approach, but ducks still tend to follow the natural flight pattern to land into the wind.

Too much or too little wind also has an effect. When the wind really gets to howling, an old waterfowling adage is to place decoys on the lee side of points of land, islands, or bays—any sheltered area. On windless days, try to pick points of land to garner any wind available. A number of motion creating decoys are available to create waves on windless days. Many also simulate moving or flying birds.

Following is a scenario for decoy sets for a fixed blind with four different wind directions. Wind is rarely straight out of the four corners of the compass, however, and decoys should be set accordingly.

WIND LEFT TO RIGHT IN FRONT OF THE BLIND

Ducks come in to land crossing in front of the blind from the right. This is the easiest set for most right-hand gunners, as the swing is more natural. Make the set with the open throat of the J or C facing to the right. Make the majority of the set somewhat to the left of the blind in order to provide plenty of landing room with an easy swing for the gunners. Leave a few decoys in front of the blind as confidence decoys.

Wind Left to Right in Front of the Blind

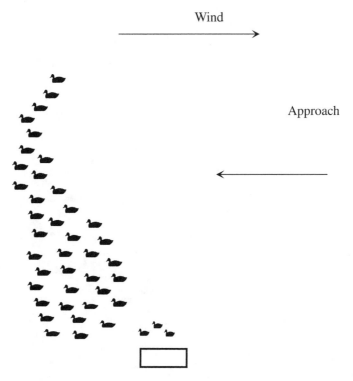

Reading and setting decoys according to the wind is the single most important factor in decoy sets. If the wind changes, don't hesitate to reset the decoys.

WIND RIGHT TO LEFT IN FRONT OF THE BLIND

This set is basically created in reverse, and that makes this wind direction a bit harder for right-handed shooters. Setting the decoy set closer to the front of the blind creates a short-stopping situation with less follow-through to the right needed for shooting. If several people are in the blind, however, don't move the set so close those on the right-hand side of the blind don't get shots.

WIND FROM DIRECTLY IN BACK OF THE BLIND

This is both the easiest and one of the hardest of decoy sets. The set is easy to construct—simply turn the J or C with its back to the blind, creating more of a

Wind Right to Left in Front of the Blind

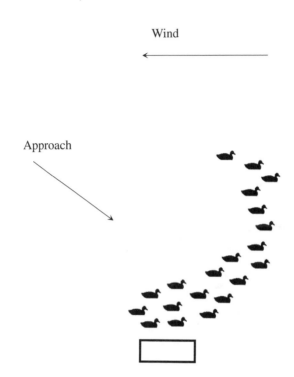

Wind

Approach

V-opening directly in front of the blind. Group all decoys as close to the blind as possible, with the decoys on the outside corners about 30 yards out. Ducks don't like to land in close to the land, even in wind situations like this, and will often land just outside the decoys, then swim into the pocket. Placing the outer decoys closer to the blind tends to draw them in closer. Shooting is fairly easy, more like dove hunting, as gunners can watch the birds come in. Dropping birds, however, are not easy to hit, and most gunners shoot over them. As the ducks can see you from a long way out on their approach, especially on open water, a well-camouflaged blind is extremely important. It's also necessary for everyone in the blind to remain motionless until the birds are directly in the pocket. It's a good idea to appoint the most knowledgeable gunner as a shooting caller. That person can watch the birds and call the shots when the birds are in position.

Wind from Directly in Back of the Blind

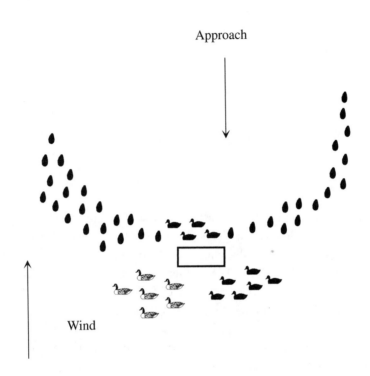

Approach

Wind

WIND DIRECTLY IN YOUR FACE

This is the hardest decoy set to create. Typically, ducks come in high over the land, over your blind, then land some distance out in the water, usually well out of shooting range. About the only tactic is to position a "raft" of decoys directly in front of the blind and about 50 to 60 yards out. Use a C- or V-shape with wings extending back on either side to about 35 yards from the blind and creating a pocket. Hopefully the ducks will not overfly the raft and land on the opposite side. If they do, keep moving the set out. Place a half dozen confidence decoys on either side of the blind next to the shore. Position a couple

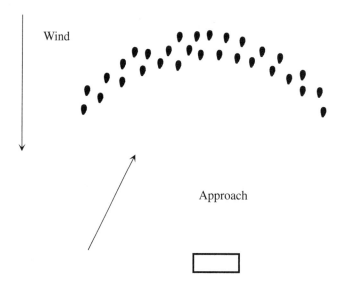

dozen or more field decoys around and behind the blind. Goose decoys positioned behind the blind as confidence decoys can also help. Shots can be complicated, as the birds normally come in high and, if they decoy, drop immediately in front of the blind. Most gunners shoot over the birds, and it's not uncommon to pick up a few rattling decoys after an in-the-face wind session.

I remember a hunt a few years ago with a direct wind in the face with gusts up to 40 mph that produced some of the most challenging duck hunting I've experienced in almost half a century of gunning. The day was the continuance of a storm generated in the Dakotas and extending all the way to Missouri. The ducks were flight ducks, eager to get to rest, but fighting extremely bad wind and weather. They came in high and fast from behind the blind, often completely overshooting the small pond we were hunting. In this instance we actually had to turn around and shoot behind the blind. Any ducks missed were gone within seconds after they crossed over our blind.

TOUGH DUCKS

Some years the ducks get tough. This usually results from weather patterns that halt migrations, causing concentrations of local ducks. "Local" ducks are the toughest, as they quickly learn to avoid the prime spots hunters use, and become call- and decoy-shy. Tough ducks aren't, however, impossible; they just require more effort and a little adjustment.

LOCATING

Some years there are fewer ducks. Not only can the weather patterns halt migrations, but more water locally has only added to the problem. Tough ducks quickly learn to hide in places with less pressure. Constant scouting is required to keep on the ducks when they're pressured. Pressured ducks frequent one spot today, another spot tomorrow. A common tactic these ducks use to avoid hunters is to raft in big groups in the middle of large lakes and reservoirs. They're really tough to hunt, but they still have to eat. Watch the rafts from a distance with binoculars and follow them to locate feeding grounds. You may have better success hunting feed fields rather than the water.

"With conditions like that, you must have more places to hunt; you can't limit yourself," said Tom Matthews. "You've got to put your places in rotation. You just can't hunt them every day and consistently have good hunting. However, our rule is if you've got 'em, hunt 'em. If you don't have them, you have to manage them. If you have a field, marsh, or timbered area that the ducks are really attracted to, there's no reason to try to conserve them, especially during tough duck seasons. Hunt them every single minute while they're there. But if your hunting dwindles quickly, pick up your decoys and don't hunt the area for two or three days. Everybody else is hunting, and if you don't hunt, your area will build up a little population again. One of the cheapest insurances is to have several good feeding fields. These fields should be scattered over a wide area to provide more opportunities as well."

"When we have a lot of water that scatters the birds," said expert waterfowler Tommy Akin from Tennessee, "I move around a lot more than usual; try to find spots the birds are using that are kind of out of the ordinary, areas that are usually dry. When the birds don't migrate until late in the season, then they often still have plenty of food on the refuges, and that's where they stay."

CALLING

When the competition becomes hard on tough ducks, good calling is a must. Most experts cut back on loudness, frequency, and even intensity when this occurs. "One unusual calling tactic we sometimes use at the last part of the season when we have those birds that don't want to leave the refuge, is a lot of goose calls on the ducks," said Akin. "Even if we don't have any geese in the area. We may put out five dozen goose floaters. On those calm and cloudy days we just do very little clucking on goose calls. We might blow a duck call when we see them get up in the distance, just to get their attention. We've got boys who can blow duck calls as good as any in the world, but you could blow your brains out on these tough ducks and they just get so close, then they peel off and don't pay any attention."

DECOYING

Only the best and most realistic decoys should be used. Time-worn decoys must be repainted and revamped. I've been using G & H decoys for many years, primarily due to their realistic appearance. I especially like the models with the movable heads to add a more natural look to the spread. This year I also added some Flambeau dekes to my spread, again because of their extremely realistic appearance. I used their Enticer Full-Body mallards on the edges of ice and on the shoreline near my blind. These full-bodied decoys add more variety. Their photorealism Pontoon Perimeter decoys are finished with an extremely realistic photo print. I also added a half dozen of their Ducks Unlimited Goose Floaters to my spread as confidence decoys.

Motion decoys can work at times. I experimented with the Expedite International remote-controlled Lucky Duck and had good luck attracting ducks early in the season. Once the local ducks are accustomed to blind locations and decoy spreads, the deadly flapping-wing decoys can, however, become the opposite of an attractant. This is particularly so with the nonremote models. Driving back home to Missouri from a hunt near Stuttgart, Arkansas, I was amazed at the number of rotating-wing decoys. And you could spot them from the highways, often a mile away.

"We also put out little bunches of pintails," said Akin. "Maybe two or three in a hole, and that helped on the mallards as well."

CAMOUFLAGE

"Concealment is a must for tough ducks," added Akins, "whether you are in a pit, blind, or standing along a tree. Those tough ducks really seem to zero in on movement." Regardless of whether boat, water, or shore blind, it must blend in perfectly with the surroundings. For marsh and shorelines with grass and reeds, Mossy Oak Shadow Grass is excellent. For flooded timber hunting I use Break-Up or Shadow Branch. As the season progresses most blinds become well worn. If on the shore or a ground blind, this includes the trampled path to the blind as well as most of the vegetation around the blind. Avoid damaging vegetation as much as possible. Regrass or recamouflage as the season progresses. I use Avery camo blind material in bulk to patch worn spots, then add natural materials. I also use Avery Real Grass and FastGrass for total blind concealment where the blinds are in full-grass situations. If you're hunting places where oaks are abundant, branches or saplings of black oaks will keep their leaves on through the season, and can be used to break up outlines.

Movement in the blind spooks already wary ducks, especially the movement made by faces looking up at the ducks. Make sure the top of the blind is well covered, and have only the more experienced hunter watch the ducks and make the call for the shots. Camouflage face masks and gloves for all hunters can also help.

OTHER DUCK TACTICS

I would rather call ducks to the dekes than waterfowl hunt in any other manner. But when the ducks don't come to me, I go to the ducks. The last week of one season saw good numbers of waterfowl rafting on the larger reservoirs during the night, then flying out to numerous farm ponds and small lakes. They fed in fields close to the ponds, then spent the day loafing on the ponds. My son Michael and I scouted the farms near a lake, got permission to hunt the ponds, and then went jump shooting. I was training a new Lab and kept her heeled by my side as we stalked the ponds. Missy soon got the idea, and it was fun to watch her creep along with us. We also took along a half dozen decoys, and once the flight was spooked from the pond, we threw out the decoys and waited a half hour or so. We discovered that with good camouflage clothing we could sit still and often get a few ducks back.

Another tactic is getting away from the normal hunting areas. Float hunting small rivers and creeks is one method. Many times ducks in these waters don't get as much pressure as the more traditional waterfowling spots. This is a particularly good tactic when other waters, such as lakes and marshes, freeze over.

If the ducks won't come to you, go to them. Jump shooting ducks off ponds and creeks can be fun and productive.

PRO TIPS

"If hunting from a shore blind, a dog is a necessity to retrieve cripples," said Mark Burch. "It's extremely important to get those wounded ducks before they have a chance to swim away and hide in the grass and brush."

"Don't be afraid to move around on big waters," said Mark Bussard. "Often it's a lot like bass fishing: Find the ducks first—then the collecting becomes easy. If you aren't getting any ducks, pull up stakes and scout new territory. With many reservoirs in the hundreds of thousands of acres, ducks can frequent any number of places."

Retrievers can make waterfowling more pleasurable and productive, eliminating the cripples that can get away.

16

ADVANCED GOOSE HUNTING STRATEGIES

The sun slowly crept above the distant tree line, creating diamond sparkles on the frost covering the foxtail weeds and cut cornstalks. As the sky became golden, thousands of big Canada geese slowly lifted from the mist-shrouded water of the refuge before us. The sound started low then built to a din as the huge dark forms milled about in the sky.

"Time to go to work," said Harold Knight with a grin. With that he began a series of loud bleating calls and began waving a huge black flag above the edge of the sunken concrete blind. David Hale mimicked his efforts on the opposite side of the bunkerlike blind.

"Looks like we got a look," said Harold during a pause in his feverish calling.

"No, they're turning back," lamented David.

Both began calling even more excitedly, still waving the flags furiously.

"They're turning back, they see us," said David excitedly. He began a series of loud double clucks imitating the excited clucks made by feeding birds and smiled at the answering clucks made by the geese headed our way. They were less than a quarter mile away now and ever so slowly closing the distance.

"Easy now," said Harold as the geese drifted within a couple of hundred yards.

As the calling shifted to short gabbles and clucks, I unconsciously fingered the stock of my Remington 1100 and peered cautiously out at the 300 or so decoys surrounding our sunken blind. The flags were stilled by the callers, but the wind-sock decoys were moving back and forth convincingly.

"Take 'em," yelled Harold. I quickly shouldered my gun, took aim at a big black-and-gray form hovering just in front of the blind, and pulled the trigger. Moments later we were excitedly pounding each other on the back, hefting our fat prizes, and reliving the action.

"Thought we were going to lose them for a moment," said David.

"Great calling," I complimented my hunting partners.

"Those flags also helped a great deal," added Harold. "If you can get their attention with the flags when they first come off the refuge, you'll almost always get them committed."

FLAGGING FOR CANADA GEESE

The hunt took place in a private blind overlooking the Tennessee National Refuge. I had visited David and Harold to learn the double-clucking sounds produced by their goose calls. I not only was impressed by the calling, but learned more about the techniques of flagging for Canada geese.

The tactic is extremely popular and effective, although it's not new. Flagging probably has been done in one form or another since geese have been hunted. It's a deadly technique, yet quite simple.

"How many times have you crawled out of your blind in boredom only to have geese come in while you're stranded outside?" asked Harold. "The reason is movement. Flagging with flags, flapping paddles, decoys that move, and even gooselike kites all provide movement and attract wary geese from a distance.

"I first saw flagging on the Chesapeake Bay in Maryland many years ago, then started doing it myself. I've always known movement in decoys was important regardless of whether hunting ducks or geese. If you watch a flock of geese feeding in a field every so often you'll see one goose reach up and stretch their wings or make a movement. Or you'll see one run at another. That's what flagging imitates, the movement made in a flock of geese. I like to hunt in a pit below ground level and have decoys all around me so I can stick the flag up in them and wave it around in a figure-8 position like an old goose flapping his wings.

"Many folks think you should quit flagging when the geese are coming in, but I've flagged until the geese were shot. I've also put the flag down when the geese were about 100 yards out and let them come in. Regardless, I don't stop flagging until I'm sure they are committed to coming in. It depends a lot on the different places you hunt. In some blinds they may commit themselves at a 100 yards, others at 200 yards.

"I also like two flags in the pit, especially when you have a long pit. One flagger on each end provides even more movement and prevents the geese from concentrating on one flagger."

Any number of items may be used for flagging geese. The most popular with Harold and other Tennessee hunters is an ordinary black cloth sewn to a piece of dowel rod. Each flagger holds one or two of the flags and moves them in a circular motion. Another type of handheld flag is a flapper. Early ones were made of Masonite and shaped like goose wings with handles cut in them.

Flagging, or waving black or white flags, depending on the species, is an excellent tactic for attracting geese.

Commercial flappers are made of plastic and are lighter weight and easier to handle. Regardless of the type used, they're extremely effective on both windy and still days and on flights from 2 to 200 birds.

Creating movement is not limited to handheld flags. A wide number of other movement-creating devices are also available.

One of the most effective is the wind-sock decoy. Bill Harper, former president of Lohman Manufacturing Company, and one of the country's top goose hunters, introduced me to the North Wind Company wind-sock decoys years ago when they first came out. More than once they provided the final touch to entice wary Canada geese from the famous Swan Lake Refuge in north Missouri. These decoys are basically a hollow bag made of lightweight fabric imprinted with a goose pattern. They are slipped over a stick pushed into the ground and a plastic goose head fitted down over the stick.

If using full-bodied field decoys, some, such as those from Higdon and G & H, offer movement decoys. Plastic wings, such as those from Flapperz, are available that can also be fastened on full-bodied decoys.

The ultimate movement creators for attracting geese long distances, however, are decoy kites, such as those from Jackite. These are simply light-weight kites fashioned and imprinted to simulate flying geese. The String-O-Wings from Nelson Outdoors create the semblance of a flying flock of geese. The string includes six 48-inch birds spanning 42 feet.

One of the problems that has developed with goose hunting is the continuing education of wary honkers and their inclination to avoid anything that even resembles a fake setup. For that reason, many serious goose hunters, particularly in heavily hunted areas, have resorted to continually growing decoy spreads and the task of providing ultrarealism to their spreads. This often entails using taxidermy-mounted birds. Great realism, but they are costly, heavy, and require constant attention. Due to the wariness of hard-hunted birds, most goose guides and hunters have also developed a "head-in-the-ground" attitude that hunters have to be completely concealed to the point that they can't even see the geese when they're right in the decoys. This provides poor shooting and crippling at best.

Flagging provides just the opposite—a chance to see all the action and get ready for the best shot. Most proponents of flagging tactics don't try to hide. If a pit blind is used, flaggers stand up waving the flags and watch the birds come right on in. Some flaggers don't even worry about the hassle of a blind.

Covering themselves with camouflage material, they sit on the ground and flag away.

Another tactic involves digging a small hole just deep enough to sit down on the edge and place your feet in the hole. This provides comfortable sitting and easy shooting, yet gets your profile low. Group big, full-bodied decoys around the hunters. A big, full-bodied decoy placed in front of each hunter also helps; then it's a matter of matching camouflage covering to the situation whether hunting cornfields or snow-covered grain fields.

A number of lightweight, one-man, lay-down blinds are also available, and most have holes in the sides for flagging.

Flagging is most effective during those times when goose movement is usually a problem, such as those bluebird days. Bright sunny weather provides the best distant viewing and action. A light breeze helps with all types of flags. The worst day for flagging tactics is a slow, drizzly, or foggy day. Cloth flags become wet and hard to work, they're hard for geese to see any distance, and even the commercial wind-sock decoys sag and look uninviting.

HARD-HUNTED SNOWS AND BLUES

The sound began as a murmur. A couple of miles away geese, thousands of them, slowly began to lift off the big irrigation lake. As more geese left the lake, the noise rose in a crescendo, and we could see the huge flock milling the lake in giant waves. Against the early-morning sky thousands of geese finally began to turn our way, and we hunkered farther down in the weeds of the fencerow, our white decoys glowing pink in the early-morning sun.

"Here they come," breathed J. T. Uptegrove. "Look at that."

The geese had formed up into a huge undulating wave coming directly at us. I fingered the safety on my old Remington 1100. Two hundred yards, 150 yards, just a few moments more and I would let the safety off. I was focused on the lead goose. Then my heart sank. The lead geese simply shifted a bit away from us and our decoys, staying out about 100 yards, just out of shooting distance. The entire line of geese undulated in the exact same manner, like a giant conga line. Frustrated, we watched the huge flock fly by then circle and land in the center of the green wheat field and about 200 yards from us. There were so many geese it took all of 10 minutes for the entire flock to settle and begin their steady work of eating our farmer friend out of business.

Hunting snows and blues takes a lot of hard work. The huge flocks typically roost on big water, then can fly great distances to feed fields. It's a matter of watching and following the flock from their refuge to the feed fields.

"Now what?" questioned my son Michael.

"We're going to sneak up and surround them," I replied with a grin.

"Yeah, right," J. T. returned. "Three hunters and about 10,000 geese. That's a heck of a lot of eyeballs."

We made battle plans and went in three different directions, hoping when we made our "squeeze stalks" the geese would fly over someone. Thirty minutes, a muddy belly-crawl later, and I was about 150 yards from the flock. In a deafening roar the entire flock suddenly leaped into the air. They started to turn my way, then circled back in the opposite direction. I watched as the flock hurriedly moved away toward, hopefully, Michael or J. T. Then I heard shots and saw one single white goose tumble to the ground.

"Not a very good average," J. T. grumbled when we met in the center of the field and examined Michael's single snow goose.

That's the problem with snows and blues. They're extremely wary, travel in big flocks, normally land and feed only in the center of big open fields, raft at night on big lakes, and tend to avoid anything with cover.

Then be there the next morning with all the decoys you can tote and white camouflage.

These wary geese are also their own worst enemy. "Light" geese, which include lesser snow (both the white and blue phase) and Ross's geese, have grown so numerous they are damaging their nesting habitat. Wildlife biologists say that without a decrease in their population, the birds could cause permanent ecological damage to themselves and other species.

Habitat improvements and changes in agricultural practices along the birds' migratory route have also contributed to explosive growth in snow goose numbers. North American snow goose numbers have tripled since the 1960s to a population of about 5 million, too many for the fragile Canadian Arctic nesting grounds to support.

The birds, which pull up plant roots when aboveground vegetation is exhausted, literally are eating away Arctic tundra habitat. A third of the area was so overgrazed in 2000 that biologists believe it is unlikely to recover in our lifetime. Wildlife biologists say a 50 percent reduction in the snow goose population is needed to prevent the birds from destroying all of the nesting area. They say the best way to accomplish this is through hunting.

A conservation order, approved by Congress since 1999, allows hunters to take snow geese beyond the regular hunting season. State wildlife agencies in the Central and Mississippi Flyways are also being allowed to use methods normally prohibited.

During the conservation order season, hunters may use electronic calls, unplugged shotguns, and shoot until a half hour after sunset with no daily bag limit. Check local regulations.

Warning: During the regular goose season all regular waterfowl (including goose) regulations are in effect. The limit on light geese, however, is quite generous.

Snow geese, however, can be had. It just takes a lot of decoys, special gear, and lots of hard work. Because the geese pull up new winter wheat, one of their favorite foods, you usually won't have any trouble getting permission to hunt them, once you locate a flock.

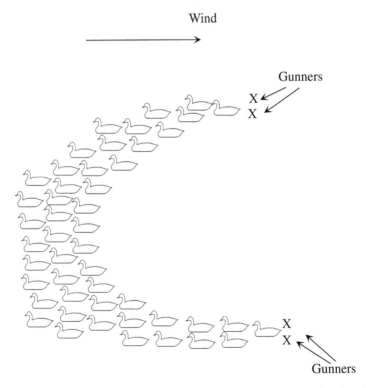

Kevin Howard likes to place gunners out on the ends of the V decoy spread rather than in the center for snows and blues. But it's important for gunners to shoot only forward.

"Get a good electronic call if hunting the spring season," said Kevin Howard, of Elsberry, Missouri. Kevin has hunted snows from Canada to Texas. "One season the guys brought big, 12-inch speakers and they really helped. Even then we had geese that would circle then veer off. One of the guys grabbed one of the speakers and kept it pointed at them and that really made a difference."

Snow geese move every day and you have to be mobile, traveling the roads, looking for feeding flocks.

Then it takes a truckload of decoys. "I've hunted with 500 to 2,500 decoys," said Howard. "And for the most part, the more the better. You can't have all full-bodied decoys. You'll need lots of silhouettes and flags, the more economical and easier-to-transport decoys. It's important to place your best decoys in the area you think the geese are going to land.

"Snow geese tend to go in a long line, and one of the best setups I've seen is an arrow shape. This has a point going out and then it flares out into a long rectangle. You leave a spot in the middle of the bottom for them to land. Then we place shooters on both sides and above the point. It's important to keep your line of fire so you are all basically shooting away from the decoy spread, and each other."

Concealment is fairly easy, as most expert snow goose gunners dress completely in white and lie on the ground right in the decoy spread. "If there's a situation where you can use a ditch line or something, we use that," added Kevin. "Sometimes the geese will come in but they won't finish that last 100 yards, especially if they've been hunted a lot. In that case we set the decoy spread up as before and keep somebody in the spread calling. We then place hunters out maybe 100 yards ahead of the spread, and in camouflage clothing. This is especially effective if the geese are coming in low enough to shoot for some distance, but then flare right before they get to the decoys."

Kevin has represented Winchester for a long time and suggests BB or BBB in Winchester Supreme High Velocity for loads. "Because you're often stretching the shots out quite a bit."

Snow goose hunting is a group situation—the more the merrier. One reason is that it takes a lot of effort to set out all the decoys. And the more guns, the better the chances for success. You normally only get one shot at snow geese, so you're not spending an entire day waiting for action. All this spells "fun" for kids. Kids can help with the chores as well as enjoy the action. Two important rules with youngsters. First, make sure they have plenty of warm clothing. Second, position the youngster and yourself so you can watch and coach the shooting. With thousands of geese milling overhead, things can get mighty exciting.

PRO TIPS

"Most people overcall Canada geese," said Tommy Akin. "You've got to get their attention when they're far away, but when you have them coming to you and looking pretty good, you don't have to put in all that championship, fancy jazz to them. You cluck, double cluck, and simply keep their attention zeroed in on your decoys. That works a whole lot better than calling your brains out. Granted, there are times when the wind is blowing when you need to do a lot more calling, but when you're hunting around a refuge or have new birds coming in, I think you can definitely overcall geese."

"I really hunt snow geese a lot," said Allan Stanley, Avery Outdoors pro staffer. "I've found it's best early, like in October, and then again late in January, February, and March. The reason is because most people aren't hunting those times. Duck season is also over. When duck season is open, there are too many people out hunting and it tends to spook the geese to death. They just don't decoy well with so much activity."

"Most people overcall Canada geese," said Tommy Akin.

17

HUNTING SEA DUCKS

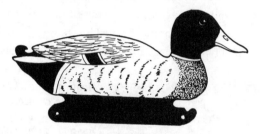

Hunting sea ducks is a totally different world than many waterfowlers experience. Sea ducks are fairly large, short, and heavy ducks. They are mostly seen at sea or along the coasts, rarely inland. During the winter months the ducks often form large rafts of mixed species, feeding on mollusks. The ducks include the scoter, black, surf, and white-winged. The scoters are deep-sea diver ducks and are commonly silent. The white-winged scoter was sometimes called the "coot" in New England. An old-fashioned New England "coot shoot" consisted of observing the direction of the flights and simply rowing out and pass shooting the birds. Scoters fly in long wavering lines.

Another coastal duck is the harlequin. Somewhat smaller than most scoters, the harlequin ducks often are found with scoters and are also usually silent. Oldsquaws—these days named the more politically correct long-tailed ducks—are also deep-diving sea ducks found on both coasts. Long-tailed ducks also form large rafts on open seas and bays and fly mostly at night. Long-tailed ducks give a piercing high-pitched yodeling sound, but I don't know of a manufacturer offering calls for them.

The eiders are far northern ducks, often abundant but only in local areas. The eiders include the common, king, spectacled, and Stellar's.

Following is advice from three expert sea duck hunters.

"The ducks I hunt here on the coast include the oldsquaw, which has a bit of a controversial name, the eiders and scoters," said Kevin Murray with L. L. Bean, in Freeport, Maine. "Those are the main ducks and they are very, very tough birds, particularly the eiders. I like to describe them as bowling balls with wings because when you pick one up, for their size, they're just so much heavier than other ducks. I think they're very tough because of all their swimming and diving and all that. They're very hard to kill. You always want to be ready with a second shot after you knock one down.

"Typically the eiders and oldsquaw ducks stay out in the deeper water, away from the mainland. They can be anywhere from just coming out of a river to 400 yards out, to 5 miles or more out. They're very deep divers that eat fish, mollusks, and that type of thing. You just have to find a ledge or an island

Hunting sea ducks may just be the ultimate challenge. The conditions are tough and dangerous, and the hunting can be challenging. (Photo courtesy Quaker Boy)

because they will come up close to islands that have very deep ledge drop-offs, or even little rock ledges that come up out of the water. You can set up on those rock ledges for pretty good success.

"It's also very effective to set up in some sort of a duck hunting boat. With this tactic you have the decoys strung out behind the boat. I actually split the decoy string in half so you have two strings of nine decoys. I've found it helps to use the correct species for the ducks you're targeting, to a lesser degree. You can use oldsquaw decoys to pull in eiders as well. But normally I also use from 12 to 18 or more eider decoys. Basically I string them up in a line of nine or so decoys.

"Preparation ahead of time is really important for setting out eider decoys. You need to have the stringers ready to go and not have to do so much messing around in the dark. We use a clip system. You just clip right onto the main trolling line. You go 4 or 5 feet and just clip on another decoy. If using the line offshore, instead of a boat, you need to anchor both ends if you're going to be in a swinging tide. You may have to adjust the rig as the tide turns.

"I don't use calls. The sea ducks aren't talkers, so I don't call. Hunting them is more visual than anything. But a lot of times I run a flag to get their attention. They come into a flag pretty good. For the most part it's pass shooting. Occasionally you'll get one of them to plop right in, but usually when they do you're not ready for it. Typically, it's pass shooting as they go by."

"The sea ducks where I hunt, which is mostly on the Delaware Bay, are primarily scoters," said Allen Stanley, Avery pro staffer. "The black, surf, and white-winged scoters. We also get a few oldsquaws, but they're not very common in our area.

"My scoter decoys didn't start out as scoter decoys. They started out as mallards, black ducks, canvasbacks, bluebills, or something. The paint got so bad on them and I got so tired of painting them as mallards that I just painted them up as scoters. I painted them up as all three species and have them on eight strings of eight decoys each. I put the strings out in a pattern that will leave a hole for the birds to pitch into. In Delaware we have to be a half mile offshore to hunt the sea ducks. There are no blinds out there, you can't have stationary blinds in the Delaware Bay, so you're hunting out of an anchored boat. I always try to camouflage the boat and hide in it, but I'm not sure that's really important. If you can make it look like a fishing boat, great, because the ducks are used to seeing fishing boats. These birds haven't been extremely wary. Now that they're being hunted more, they have become more wary.

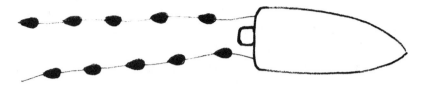

Sets for sea ducks are normally rigged on gang or "toll" lines behind the boat.

They do, however, definitely come into the decoys. They know how to decoy better than probably anything. I've always wanted to come up with some calls for them, but I never have. I don't think calling is a factor for hunting these ducks. It's pretty much being where they want to feed. I like to be set up by daylight. Where we hunt is not very deep water, 6 to 12 or 15 feet deep. I also prefer to flag to get their attention instead of trying to call them. Flagging works really well. If it's early in the morning, and it's rough, you're only going to see some of the decoys riding on top of the waves at any one time, so it's hard for the ducks to pick out the decoys. I lie in the boat, wave the flag, and get their attention. Once they spot the decoys, you don't have to flag. Just get ready to shoot."

Ernie Calendrelli, director of public relations for Quaker Boy Game Calls, in Niagara Falls, hunts sea ducks on Lake Ontario. Ernie targets oldsquaw and white-winged scoter. "They're pretty easy," said Ernie. "I have a 19-foot Lund boat. I put a 40-yard decoy line off one of my gunwales, depending on the wind direction. I run the farthest decoy at 40 yards and I only run six decoys. I turn the engine the right way and simply drift with the wind. Most of the hunting is pass shooting where the birds are passing over the tops of the decoys. But a lot of times the birds will cup and come into the decoys."

PRO TIPS

"It's a very, very cold, windy, and wet sport," said Kevin. "The water is almost always rough because you're out in the open ocean. It can get very, very rough. You need to be very careful and make sure your equipment is running well."

18

INTRODUCING KIDS TO WATERFOWLING

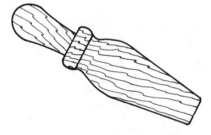

Momma was glaring across the dinner table at me, but son Mark didn't seem to notice. "It was so cold we had to pour coffee on the dog to get him unstuck from the ice," Mark excitedly exclaimed. Later that evening I explained to Joan that her son, then nine years old, had been perfectly safe, and that maybe in his excitement, Mark had exaggerated about how cold it had been. Now a grown man, Mark is still one of the most devout waterfowlers I've had the pleasure of hunting with, and he has been a waterfowl guide for a number of years. It all, however, began many years ago.

Waterfowling is one of the best of hunting sports to introduce youngsters to for a number of reasons. First, you can control many of the factors, with comfort being number one. Mark hadn't been cold because he was bundled in lots of clothes, and we were hunting out of a blind with a heater. These days it's even easier to keep your young companions warm due to the number of high-tech clothing options and even boots available that are made to fit youngsters. It's important the clothing fits properly, especially the boots. Too large a boot creates air pockets and cold; plus, they're hard to walk in. Too small a boot allows the foot to compress the insulation and again creates cold. I've had the pleasure of hunting with a number of youngsters since introducing Mark to waterfowling, and the major complaint is cold feet—but that's often the major complaint of adults as well. Make sure the young have gloves, caps, and even face protectors that fit as well. And take along some handwarmers. Most importantly, when they get cold, take them home, or at least to a vehicle or camp to allow them to warm up. Do this even if the ducks are flying fast and furious. Staying cold is a definite discouragement.

Mark's first hunts were in snug blinds, but as he got older we hunted out of boat blinds, which are a bit more dangerous, as well as harder work, though at times are the most productive. When Mark was 16 he really wanted to hunt

Waterfowling is a great sport for introducing youngsters to hunting.

with other youngsters his own age. One morning I got one of those 4:00 A.M. calls all parents fear. It, however, wasn't an accident or serious trouble; he had gotten my four-wheel-drive pickup stuck on a backcountry road leading down in to Stockton Reservoir, one of his favorite duck hunting spots.

It's also important to take along plenty of food, especially when hunting with younger children. Chocolate chip cookies and piping-hot cocoa are hard to beat. And you don't have to feel guilty about taking along those candy bars you've been hoarding. When the ducks aren't flying you can always eat. I've found youngsters often ask what there is to eat even before all the decoys are out.

Probably the single best factor in hunting with youngsters is the companionship. When you're stuck in a blind waiting for the next flight, you'll learn a lot about your kids, and they may learn some things about you as well. When the ducks aren't flying, kids can move around in a duck blind. This is an important factor and the reason waterfowling is easier for youngsters than sitting on a deer stand for long hours while attempting to not move.

Waterfowling also provides the opportunity for a great deal of learning about the outdoors. If you pay attention, there's almost always something going on — from the wren that visits the blind to an occasional beaver, muskrat, or other game that inhabits the waterfowler's world. Then there are the waterfowl themselves. A wide range of waterfowling exists from the early teal season, and all the different duck species including divers, puddlers, and sea ducks. Then there's goose season; kids are always impressed by the size of a goose in hand.

Another reason kids like waterfowling is the active nature of the sport. You're constantly doing something — putting out decoys, then calling to attract the ducks and geese. Dogs make up a good part of waterfowling, and for the most part kids and dogs go together like cake and ice cream. Some working dogs, however, can be surly toward everyone. Be careful of any dogs you are not familiar with.

Make sure youngsters have their own call and help them learn to use it. Guaranteed that will make them interested in hunting waterfowl. You may, in fact, find your young companion quickly becoming more adept at calling than many of your adult hunting buddies. Kids take to calling really fast because they don't have any hang-ups about sounding bad.

Shooting from a blind or boat can be dangerous, even for adults, so you probably need to first introduce younger children without having them carry a

Waterfowling is fun; there's the chance for camaraderie with family or friends, there's the companionship of the dog, and there's always some sort of wildlife activity.

gun. As they become older, and learn basic gun safety and handling, you can allow them to carry a gun and shoot at waterfowl. It's hard to say at what age they should start carrying a gun and shooting—it depends on the youngster. Shooting out of a boat or blind is more difficult than standing and shooting, so you should practice with them in a hunting situation before the season. Use a hand thrower to toss a few clay pigeons so they get the feel of shooting from awkward positions.

Make sure the gun fits the youth properly. Many parents make the mistake of providing a youngster with a .410 single-shot gun. Actually the best choice is a 20-gauge pump, and several companies make these guns in youth models with shortened stocks. The 20-gauge provides a better pattern for youngsters and thus better chances for success. Success is also a major key to keeping youngsters interested in the sport. The pump-action shotgun doesn't kick as hard as a straight-action gun, and as the shell has to be pumped in place, there's more safety than with an automatic. By all means make sure the youngster understands proper and safe shooting techniques and ethics when shooting from a blind or boat. Blinds can create extremely loud gun reports; you should consider hearing protection for everyone in the blind as well.

Make sure you involve the youngster in the dressing and cleaning of the waterfowl. I've never, however, found that a problem. In fact, most youngsters are naturally intrigued by the dressing process, especially if they start early. And be sure to cook and serve that waterfowl as soon after the hunt as possible. The youngster should be involved in the entire hunting process—from planning, preseason decoy preparation, and preseason trapshooting practice to the actual hunts, followed by the equally important dressing, cleaning, and cooking.

Try it—introduce your children, or someone else's children, to the pleasures of waterfowling. You'll probably find you gain more than they do.

WATERFOWL
SOURCES

Ace Decoy Anchors, 662–227–1250, www.decoyweights.com

Advantage Camouflage, 800–992–9968, www.advantagecamo.com

Alumacraft, 507–931–1050, www.alumacraft.com

Ameristep, 800–374–7837, www.ameristep.com

API Outdoors, 800–228–4845, www.apioutdoors.com

The Arthur Armstrong Duck Boat Company, 800–213–8428, www.tdbco.com

Avery Outdoors, 800–333–5119, www.averyoutdoors.com

BBK Enterprises, 210–637–1633, bbk@texas.net

Benelli, U.S.A. Corp., 301–283–6981, www.benelliusa.com

Beretta U.S.A. Corp., 301–283–2191, www.berettausa.com

Big Head Robotic Decoys, 570–326–5622, www.bigheaddecoys.com

Big River Game Calls, 800–922–9034, www.outlandsports.com

Bismuth Cartridge Company, 800–759–3333, www.bismuth-notox.com

Blackwater Decoy Co., 888–BW–DECOY, www.duckdecoys.com

Browning, 801–876–2711, www.browning.com

C & C Outfitters, Vernon Cooksey, 318–688–1234

Cabela's, 800–237–4444, www.cabelas.com

Carry-Lite Decoys, 501–649–5720, www.carrylitedecoys.com

Carsten's Industries, 320–256–3919, www.carstensindustries.com

The Coleman Company, 800–835–3278, www.coleman.com

Cutt Down Game Calls, 877–288–3966, www.cuttdowncalls.com

Decoy Dolly, Marshland Enterprises, 888–450–1172, www.marshlandenterprises.com

The Decoy Heart, Advanced Decoy Research, 731–658–2934, www.decoyheart.com

The Decoy Shop, 888–8–DECOYS, www.thedecoyshop.com

Duck Buggy, Trax America, 800–232–2327, www.traxamerica.com

Duck Commander, 877–396–7612, www.duckcommander.com

Duck Dock, Windsor Industries, 800–726–7437, www.duckdock.com

DuckLogic, 913–631–4774, www.ducklogic.com

Duck Wrangler Boats, 330–602–9008, www.duckwrangler.com

DukshU Decoy Anchors, Niemann & Poore Co., 877–4–DUKSHU, www.dukshu.com

Environ-Metal, 541–367–3522, www.hevishot.com

Expedite International, 715–381–2935, www.trumotion.com

EZ-Tipperz, Days Afield, 802–425–5128, www.daysafield.com

Farm Form Decoys, 409–765–6361, www.farmformdecoys.com

FastGrass, Camo Outfitters, Inc., 616–956–9551, www.camooutfitters.com

Faulk's Game Call Co., 337–436–9726

Feather Flex Decoys, Outland Sports, 800–922–9034, www.outland-sports.com

Federal Cartridge, 800–322–2342, www.federalcartridge.com

Fiber Pro, 800–536–4604, www.fiber-pro.com

Fiberdome, 800–359–4416, www.tuffyboats.com

Final Approach by Kolpin, 877–9–KOLPIN, www.kolpin.com

Fishing Hot Spots, 800–ALL–MAPS, www.fishinghotspots.com

Flambeau Products, 800–457–5252, www.flambeau.com

Flapperz, 888–33–WINGS, www.flapperz.com

Flex Tone Mallard Calls, Wiley Duck Outdoor Products, 662–324–9188, www.wileyduck.com

Foiles Migrators, 618–232–1434, www.foilesstraitmeat.com

Fowl Foolers Calls & Decoys, 800–352–5301, www.fowlfoolers.com

Franchi, 301–283–6981, www.franchiusa.com

G & H Decoys, 800–6H–DECOY, www.ghdecoys.com

Goose Noose Decoys, Inc., 636–524–6449

GooseView Industries, 800–399–5034, www.furtmanhill.com

Greenhawk Decoy Anchors, available Cabela's

H & R 1871 Inc., 978–632–9393, www.hr1871.com

Haydel's Game Calls, Inc., 800–HAYDELS, www.haydels.com

Herter's, 800–654–3825, www.herters.com

Higdon Motion Decoys, 618–524–3385, www.higdondecoys.com

Hunter's Specialties, 800–728–0321, www.hunterspec.com

Inflata-Coy Decoys, available Cabela's

Intruder, 800–553–5129, www.intruderinc.com

Ithaca Gun Works, 888–9–ITHACA, www.ithacagun.com

Iverson Calls, 888–833–8251, www.iversononline.com

Jackite, Inc., 877–JACKITE, www.flyingdecoys.com

Knight & Hale Game Calls, 800–531–1201, www.knightandhale.com

L. L. Bean Inc., 800–809–7057, www.llbean.com

Legend Craft, Inc., 501–316–4409, www.legendcraft.com

Lohman Game Calls, 800–922–9034, www.outlandsports.com

Lowe Boats, 417–532–9101, www.lowe.com

Mack's Prairie Wings, 417–532–9101, www.macksprairiewings.com

M.A.D.D. Calls, 800–922–9034, www.outlandsports.com

Mad Dog Gear by Stearns, 800–697–9801, www.stearnsinc.com

The Mallard Machine, 501–770–DUCK, www.themallardmachine.com

Mallardtone Game Calls, 309–798–2481, www.mallardtonegamecalls.com

Manco, Inc., 800–321–1733, www.manco.com, www.duckproducts.com

Mojo Mallard by HuntWise, 318–283–7777, www.mojomallard.com

O. F. Mossberg & Sons Inc., 800–989–GUNS, www.mossberg.com

Mossy Oak Brand Camouflage, 888–MOSSY–OAK, www.mossyoak.com

Nelson Outdoors LLC, 920–485–3299, www.string-o-wings.com

North Wind Outdoor Co., 800–739–4135, www.northwindoutdoor.com

Osage Canoes, 417–532–7288, www.osage-canoes.com

Otter Outdoors, 877–GO–OTTER, www.otteroutdoors.com

Outlaw Decoys, 800–688–5297, www.outlaw.com

P. S. Olt Co., 309–348–3633

Penn's Woods, 724–468–8311, www.pennswoods.com

Phoenix Poke Boat, 800–354–0190, www.pokeboat.com

Plasti-Duk, Neumann & Bennett, 800–779–0442, www.decoy1.com

Pop-Up Blinds, Innovative Wildlife Specialties, 402–454–3334, www.popupblind.com

Porta Bote International, 800–227–8882, www.porta-bote.com

Primos Hunting Calls, 800–523–2395, www.primos.com

Quaker Boy, 800–544–1600, www.quakerboygamecalls.com

Quick Pro Blind, 888–TJ–BLIND, www.quick-pro-blinds.com

The Real DeCoy, A&M Waterfowl, Inc., 800–818–4842, www.the-realdecoy.com

Real Geese, LSP-Webfoot, Sean Mann Outdoors, 419–334–4260, www.webfootdecoys.com

Realtree Camouflage, 800–992–9968, www.realtree.com

Remington, 800–243–9700, www.remington.com

RoboDuk, 877–525–9571, www.roboduk.com

Robo Duck, Chrono Mfg., 800–465–6678, www.ongaros.com

Roto Duck, Mathews Decoys, 530–742–0743, www.motormallard.com

SeaArk Boats, 870–367–5317, www.seaark.com

Semmler Products, Inc., 605–394–9373, www.semmlerinc.com

Sevylor U.S.A. Inc., 800–821–4645, www.sevylor.com

Southern Game Calls, 800–881–1964, www.southerngamecalls.com

Stoeger Industries, 301–283–6300, www.stoegerindustries.com

Sturm, Ruger & Co., Inc., 520–541–8820, www.ruger-firearms.com

Sure-Shot Game Calls, 800–643–7430, www.sureshotgamecalls.com

Tanglefree, 800–982–4868, www.tanglefree.com

Tim Grounds Championship Calls, 618–983–5649, www.timgrounds.com

Tracker Marine, 417–866–4242, www.trackermarine.com

Triton Boats, 888–8–TRITON, www.tritonboats.com

Underbrush, Shelter Pro LLC, 888–376–2004, www.underbrush-blinds.com

Waco Mfg., 501–753–2866, www.wacomfg.com

War Eagle Boats, 870–367–1554, www.wareagleboats.com

WaterQuest Boats, Leisure Life Limited, 800–552–6287, www.llboats.com

Weatherby, Inc., 800–227–2016, www.weatherby.com

Whirl-E-Gig, 650–593–4277, www.whirl-e-gig.com

Winchester Ammunition, 618–258–3340, www.winchester.com

Winchester Firearms, 801–876–3440, www.winchester-guns.com

WonderDuck Decoys, 800–876–1697, www.wonderduck.com

Woods Wise Products, 800–735–8182, www.woodswise.com

Xpress Boats, 501–262–5300, www.xpressboats.com

Decoys at Shelburne Museum by David S. Webster and William Kehoe, published by the Shelburne Museum, Shelburne, Vermont, 1961, revised edition, 1971.

INDEX